THE COMPLETE HUNTER™

500 DEER HUNTING TIPS

Strategies, Techniques & Methods

Bill Vaznis

Creative Publishing
international
Minneapolis, Minnesota

Bill Vaznis is a full-time outdoor writer and award-winning photographer whose work has appeared in every major outdoor magazine in North America, including Whitetail Strategies, Bowhunter World, Deer and Deer Hunting. *He has contributed nearly 1,200 feature articles and columns plus thousands of photographs on bow hunting, gun hunting and muzzleloading whitetail deer. This is his third book, the second on deer hunting. Bill lives in upstate New York.*

Creative Publishing
international

Copyright © 2008
Creative Publishing international, Inc.
400 First Avenue North
Suite 300
Minneapolis, MN 55401
1-800-328-3895
www.creativepub.com
All rights reserved

President/CEO: Ken Fund
Publisher: Bryan Trandem
Senior Acquisition Editor: Barbara Harold
Production Managers: Laura Hokkanen, Linda Halls
Creative Director: Michele Lanci-Altomare
Senior Design Managers: Brad Springer, Jon Simpson
Design Managers: Sara Holle, James Kegley
Book & Cover Design: Emily Brackett
Page Layout: Greg Nettles

All photos © Bill Vaznis except those © Denver Bryan, The Browning Company, Michael H. Francis, Tes Randle Jolly, Lon E. Lauber, Mark Raycroft, Ken Thommes.

Library of Congress Cataloging-in-Publication Data
Vaznis, Bill.
  500 deer hunting tips : strategies, techniques & methods / Bill Vaznis.
    p. cm.
Includes index.
  ISBN-13: 978-1-58923-352-2 (hard cover)
  ISBN-10: 1-58923-352-2 (hard cover)
  1. Deer hunting. I. Title. II. Title: Five hundred deer hunting tips.
  SK301.V38 2009
  799.2'765--dc22   2007033513

Printed in China

10 9 8 7 6 5

CONTENTS

INTRODUCTION

The white-tailed deer is North America's number one big game animal, a title that has been held since early colonial days when settlers and natives alike depended on the whitetail for food and clothing.

Today the whitetail is pursued with nearly the same vigor by bow, muzzleloader, shotgun or rifle enthusiasts across much of the region. Only now it is not a matter of life or death, but a form of relaxation that is passed on from one generation to the next.

What is a deer hunter? What skills must he or she possess? Unlike any of the ball sports, deer hunters generally become more proficient with age. Indeed, as we grow older we become more in harmony with nature and in turn better woodsmen. Shared campfires coupled with seasons of experience help us not only fine-tune our traditional strategies, but learn new tactics as well.

There is a fly in the ointment, however. In the good old days fathers and uncles would pass on their skills to their sons and nephews (and sometimes their nieces and daughters, too!), who would in turn pass on that lore to their offspring. We became better deer hunters by listening and sharing information around the campfire.

Today, that link has, in many cases, been broken. One-parent families, the anti-hunting movement and competition from skateboards and video games all add to the pressures of modern-day life. Sadly, in many cases if it were not for the printed word there would be no one to light the torch—much less pass it on.

This book offers tips that come from years of experience as well as many nights spent around those campfires.

Chapter 1

FUNDAMENTALS

Successful deer hunters, those that tag racked bucks year after year, scout for deer and deer sign every chance they get. They study topography, prevailing wind currents and available ground cover to learn where bucks hide, what they eat, where they breed and how they sneak about undetected.

To avoid pushing deer out of the area, good hunters have also learned to sneak about undetected, in part by practicing scent control and by using trail cameras to monitor deer behavior. The knowledge they gain from hours and hours afield helps them set up successful ambush sites.

EARLY-SEASON SCOUTING

Tagging a bow and arrow buck in the early deer season is definitely a rush. We seem to dream about deer and deer hunting all year long, and to be afield as the leaves are turning crimson and yellow has to be one of the highlights of anybody's bow season. Indeed, bucks are in prime physical condition prior to the rut and are more predictable now as they move like clockwork between bedding grounds and feeding areas.

Get the Lay of the Land

1

Getting a crack at a racked buck in the early season takes scouting, and in most cases plenty of it! If you are familiar with your hunting grounds, familiar enough to find your way around in poor light, then the amount of scouting needed may be only minimal. On the other hand, if you have learned the general whereabouts of a real dandy buck, but you are unfamiliar with his home area, then be sure to give yourself more time.

2

The best time to start scouting is right after the close of the deer season. Your first goal is to get a better handle on the lay of the land. This means understanding the relationships between various topographical features such as ravines, gentle slopes, plateaus, swamps and crop fields. The only way you're going to accomplish this is with plenty of shoe leather. You will suddenly realize why bucks exit a ravine along a certain ridge or why other bucks are attracted to a particular plateau or hump in a swamp.

If you are unfamiliar with your hunting grounds, take your topographical maps and aerial photos with you in the field. Studying these, you'll be surprised how fast you learn the lay of the land.

3

Your second goal is to pinpoint preferred bedding areas and major travel routes—an easy task if there is snow on the ground. Feeding areas can change from one week to the next, but good bedding areas remain more or less constant over time. Back-track trails to learn the whereabouts of these preferred bedding sites, and then mark them on one of your maps for future reference.

4

The key to finding bucks in the early season is food, and there is no better time to start locating potential food sources than springtime. I take my binoculars and glass old farmsteads, hedge rows and creek bottoms for apple blossoms during green-up. I also keep tabs on "nut" production from early spring on through summer by glassing the uppermost branches of oak, beech and hickory trees. Look for nuts seated in or surrounded by a hard woody cupule. Be aware that frosts and droughts can have a negative effect on mast production.

Believe in that old saying: Find the food, find the deer.

INSIDER INFO

One recent summer a jogger approached me as I was preparing for an evening scouting mission. He did not hunt with a bow but shared information with me about some of the bigger bucks known to inhabit the area. A double-drop-tined buck, for example, had been feeding behind his house quite regularly all summer long—a buck that I hadn't seen since the late bow season. This tidbit of information had my mind racing, for now I had a better idea where he was bedding. When I asked the jogger about a wide-racked 12-pointer that often traveled with the double-drop-tined buck, however, my heart sank. That buck had been shot opening day of shotgun season by his brother-in-law. If he hadn't told me, I would have never known what happened to the Boone & Crockett contender.

Learn to "see" rubs; some are very obvious and tell you a lot about deer in the area.

Keep a mental tally of "nut" production; it's a sure sign of a deer magnet.

5

You also want to learn which deer made it not only through the fall fusillade, but the depths of winter and any early-spring snowstorms as well. Antler drops and actual sightings of deer should help confirm your suspicions.

6

When off-season scouting, never walk the same route in or out of the woods. It is just too easy to miss an important sign.

7

Your third goal is to locate rut sign, including scrapes and rub lines, to help predict the following fall's breeding patterns. Scrape lines, for example, often appear in the same location year after year, whereas a mixture of bright and gray rubs might indicate the presence of a mature buck working the area. Rubs and scrapes can also point you in the direction of previously unknown feeding areas and bedding sites.

8

By about the Fourth of July antler growth has progressed to the point where the better bucks can certainly be singled out. Although the racks are far from "full figure," you can gauge the potential width, mass and total number of points with ease. By late summer it is not unusual to see local bucks herded into bachelor groups.

Keep in mind that mature bucks prefer the dark edges of secluded openings and rarely expose themselves in areas frequented by family groups of does and fawns. You will generally find these monarchs in adjacent fields, feeding alone just before dark. Stay until pitch black and glass the thick stuff if you want to catch a glimpse.

Keep tabs on active agriculture. The presence or absence of cash crops often dictates buck travel routes and bedding areas.

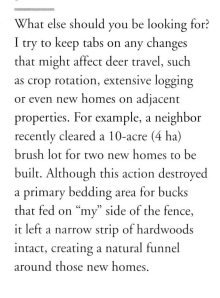

What else should you be looking for? I try to keep tabs on any changes that might affect deer travel, such as crop rotation, extensive logging or even new homes on adjacent properties. For example, a neighbor recently cleared a 10-acre (4 ha) brush lot for two new homes to be built. Although this action destroyed a primary bedding area for bucks that fed on "my" side of the fence, it left a narrow strip of hardwoods intact, creating a natural funnel around those new homes.

10

After I figure out what is new and different in my hunting area, I focus on primary food sites by learning which adjacent fields farmers are cultivating this year. This alone tells me which routes local bucks are apt to take to other available feeding sites as well as secretive bedding areas. I know, for example, that where I hunt there are two places deer cross a creek and one where they slide under an old barbed-wire fence. In an hour or so I can inspect these and a half-dozen or so other crossings for recent deer activity. Then all I have to do is stay clear of the old farm until the season opens, confident that I have several food-related options for ambush sites.

MODIFIED PLANS

I was about as ready as I was ever going to be. I put the cap back on the tube of face paint and grabbed my fanny pack before stepping out of the 4x4 and into the early-morning air. Shooting light was still over an hour away, but I was in a hurry to get up the hill and onto an abandoned logging road while it was still dark. I didn't want to spook any deer that might be feeding in a nearby 50-acre (20 ha) green field, and the old road provided a quiet pathway around the grassy opening on the downwind side.

I hurried along and was soon standing motionless on the edge of a grown-over pasture 1/2 mile (0.8 km) away, waiting for the darkness to lift. I knew bucks would eventually pass through here as they left the mix of standing cornfields and apple orchards to the east. My plan was to still-hunt through the briars and dogwood, hoping to catch one of the racked bucks I knew inhabited the farm flat-footed before he made it to one of several nearby bedding areas. I was not to be denied.

Twenty minutes later I heard a faint tick-tick-tick of two bucks sparring a short distance away. I immediately slipped an arrow out of my quiver and sneaked in a little closer. Sure enough, there were two nice 8-pointers testing each other's strength within easy bow range. I nocked a broadhead and waited for a clear shot. When it came, however, I passed. It was, after all, only the first day of bow season, and I knew there were plenty of bigger bucks on the farm.

You can scout before or during the season; alone or with a buddy.

11

If I am hunting a new farm, as I try to do every year to expand my turf, I must scout with more zeal. As I mentioned earlier, the key to locating early-season bucks is undoubtedly food. Active agriculture is an obvious source, but also look for secondary food sources that bucks utilize en route to that bean lot or plot of buckwheat, such as an old apple orchard or a cut-over filled with new growth. Bucks linger here for half an hour or so before committing themselves to their primary food source just before dark. These are excellent ambush sites for the tree stand hunter and the ground blind hunter, as well as the still-hunter.

The trick here is to slip into strategic locations, and then look for bucks as they emerge to feed in the late evening, or catch them retreating from that opening at first light.

Location Preparation

12

Once you have the general location of several bucks pegged, it's time to do some light in-field scouting. Always wear rubber boots, and make sure your human stench doesn't drift into known concentrations of deer. And even then try to do your reconnoitering in the middle of the day, preferably during or just before a rain shower to further minimize your human scent.

Your goal is to prepare several tree stand locations, ground blind ambush sites or still-hunting routes without putting any stress on the deer herd. Choose at least two evening ambush sites as well as a couple of morning sites. You want to be able to cover any contingency, from a change in wind direction to a corn lot being harvested at the last minute.

13

The biggest mistake early-season bowhunters seem to make is committing themselves to some last-minute scouting, or even worse, sitting in their tree stands during the last week or so before the opener. (You can easily push deer out of their bedding areas or off their primary food sources by spending too much time now in your deer woods.) Even spotlighting, where legal, should be avoided. No matter how quiet you are and how well you control your human odor, the bucks will know you have invaded their turf and will adjust their daily routines accordingly.

My hot spot panned-out!

14

Another mistake to avoid is to erect your stands immediately before the opener. One fall morning I scanned an old farm field just before first light to see if any deer were feeding. I had to get to the far side, so I wouldn't spook any bucks. I immediately spotted several white slashes on saplings bordering the corner of the lot. A quick look with my field glasses revealed a homemade stand, unpainted lumber and all, sticking out of the trees. If that stand stood out like the proverbial sore thumb to me, how long do you think it took for the deer to get wise to its location?

15

Don't be all fired up to hunt your hotspot opening day if the conditions are less than perfect. If the wind and weather are not to your advantage or even if you oversleep and can't get to your ambush site "on time," be smart and wait it out. After all, if you can't hunt the first day of the season, the second day of deer season will still be your first day afield!

LOCATING RACKED BUCKS

"Stop the truck!" my friend yelled as we rounded a curve in the old farm road. "Now back up to that clearing we just passed. Did you see how the creek bed slipped back around the edge of that cornfield? It looks like a natural passageway for bucks bedding on the upper ridges to sneak into the valley undetected. Now look over in the corner, near that old tractor; you can see where they've been crossing the creek. That's a great place for a tree stand!"

Soon we were both picking out likely bedding areas, feeding sites and runways on that old farm by simply glassing the old farmstead from a high point along the road and comparing our sightings with those brown squiggles found on topo maps. In an hour we knew enough about the deer on that old New York farm to start hunting the next morning.

When you know what terrain features and later what types of ground cover to look for, unraveling the whereabouts of racked bucks becomes a fun exercise.

Terrain Features

16

While scouting, one of your primary goals is to identify those bedding areas preferred by bucks during the early season and pre-rut period. Start by assuming the greatest number of bucks bed high during the day, and then feed in the lowlands under the cover of darkness. That's because thermals help bucks keep tabs on what is below, and there are fewer contacts with predators at these elevations, including humans, for them to contend with.

17

Uneven terrain features are another draw to mature deer. Try to find ravines, creek beds, deep canyons and slopes dotted with knobs and knolls on your topo map. Bucks like them in part because swirling winds quickly warn them of impending danger. One sniff is all it takes for a buck to disappear from view.

Your footing may not be so sure, but the deer have no problem moving in habitat like this.

It is easy to see how terrain features promote travel. How many buck routes can you find here? There are at least a half-dozen solid candidates.

NORMAL BUCK BEDDING AREAS

During the early season and pre-rut, unmolested bucks generally bed within 1/4 mile (0.4 km) of a preferred food source, but bucks will travel 1 mile (1.6 km) or more to feed in an alfalfa lot or a recently harvested cornfield. In farm country you can find bucks hiding in brush lots, overgrown fields, old vineyards, cornfields, heads of ravines, cattail swamps, hardwood ridges and thorn apple thickets. In wilderness areas, add high peaks, plateaus above clear-cuts, inside clear-cuts, logging slashings, river banks, beaver flows and humps inside large swamps to the list.

When the rut reaches its peak, bucks abandon these bedding sites and follow estrous does around, bedding and feeding where she beds and feeds. They rarely return to their summer and early-fall bedding areas.

In the late season you can count on bucks bedding near food sources in the thickest cover available. Winter storms, however, push them to bed under the boughs of pine, hemlock and spruce as well as brush-choked ravines and the lee sides of hills. Hillsides with a southern exposure are another good bet when winter temperatures turn bitter.

Do bucks bed in the same location day after day? Sometimes, but not always. Approaching storms, early-morning air temperatures, a change in wind direction, emerging food sources, barking dogs, spotlighters, trespassers, bird hunters and kids playing can all force a buck to bed elsewhere.

18

Another terrain feature that attracts bucks is a small island in a swamp or on a large body of water. Locate such elevated hummocks by studying topo maps or by backtracking deer in the snow after the water has frozen. These are probably the most difficult to hunt.

19

Bucks are also attracted to certain terrain features for food. Pinpointing these preferred feeding locations is not as difficult as it might seem. Begin your search by examining any blue ink on your topo map. Creek beds, shorelines surrounding ponds and lakes and, of course, the edges of swamps are all places where sunlight can reach the forest floor, producing succulent new growth.

20

Ask around—including anglers, hikers, canoeists and even your local wildlife biologist—about the presence of beaver flows. Except for a freshly constructed beaver dam, I can't recall ever scouting a beaver flow in deer country and not seeing deer sign.

21

One more terrain feature worth a scouting trip is a plateau. These, and to some degree nearby ridges, are often choice feeding locations, especially if they're situated on south-facing slopes and have an oak, hickory or beech grove present.

The food is not the only reason that deer gather here. Plateaus are easy to navigate, requiring fewer calories. They also serve as transition zones, especially if there are no nearby openings, allowing deer to congregate until it's time to continue on to their primary food source. As such, it's not uncommon to find rubs and rub lines, and scrapes and scrape lines atop a plateau.

22

The most important terrain feature to examine for a feeding location, however, is undoubtedly a large opening. In the big woods, these include beaver flows plus burns, landslides, ice slides and openings created by tornadoes, windstorms and hurricanes. Man-made openings include clear-cuts, railroad beds, power lines, gas lines and underground cable right-of-ways.

23

Openings in farm country are much easier to locate and scout. Abandoned farm fields and active agriculture are obvious choices, but how many of these prime feeding locations are shielded behind blocks of woods? If you scout primarily by driving the back roads, you will probably not be aware of these prime sites that attract undisturbed deer. To get on board, simply reexamine your topo map. Check the date along the margin, but large openings out of sight are always worth a firsthand look-see.

24

Even in relatively flat country, like Iowa or eastern Montana, give any slight elevation a look-see. If you find a concentration of rubs facing downhill with several piles of deer pellets nearby, then you have probably discovered a buck's bed.

Posting just inside a natural opening or along a hardwood ridge for hungry bucks is a good early-morning or late-afternoon strategy.

Dry humps inside swamps and along major waterways attract and hold bucks. Hunting them, however, can be difficult.

This hillside holds plenty of bucks that rely on ground cover for daytime safety zones as well as feeding areas and travel routes.

Travel Routes

25

Shorelines, creek beds and steep ravines all block a buck's forward progress. He parallels these features until he finds a suitable opening, which makes these crossings good ambush sites. The tips of bays, shallow riffles and the tops of ravines are especially productive in this regard.

26

Terrain features that promote travel include gentle slopes, spurs and saddles where bucks can save energy going up and down a hill or crossing over from one valley to the next. Ridges adjacent to steep country or sheer cliffs are another travel route bucks choose to save calories.

27

Thick tangles of various types of vegetation are a magnet for bucks seeking refuge—and the thicker and more impenetrable the better.

In the Northeast, for example, mountain laurel thickets, patches of dogwood, as well as cattails and swamp grasses, offer ideal cover. Not only do they hide a buck's form, but they make it nearly impossible for a hunter to walk through without getting tripped up.

In the South, kudzu and honeysuckle can be just as impenetrable, as can alder swamps and thorn apple thickets in the Midwest and elsewhere east of the Mississippi. Planted pine plantations and unharvested cornfields also offer superb cover.

28

The routes that really catch my eye are those steep ravines and rocky draws that would give me trouble if I dared to enter. Any place that common sense tells you to avoid is probably just the spot to catch a big buck sneaking about between his bedding area and a prime feeding location. He may also use this tangle as a conduit as he monitors one doe bedding area after another during the peak of the rut.

29

When storms approach, look for whitetails to move to bed down in alder thickets and thick stands of evergreens around swamps, or patches of dogwood and tamarack on the lee or protected side of a hill.

In winter, all deer need are a few briars and some brush to break up their outline.

30

One of the most overlooked bedding areas is created during the timber harvesting process. Slashings, a by-product of the axe and chain saw, consist of tree tops, rotten logs and other debris that big bucks bed around. Tree trunks laying askew and dead branches piled atop each other are more often than not impossible to climb through quietly. Blackberry briars, alders and replanted softwoods soon take over, offering even more cover.

31

When the weather turns brutally cold, expect bucks to again change their bedding routines and lie down as close as they dare to a major food source, such as a corn lot or near the edge of a swamp. A nearby farm field overgrown with grasses, briars, goldenrod and hardwood saplings sometimes suffices. Abandoned vineyards, such as those near my home in upstate New York, are another favorite.

32

Unlike the summer when bucks seek deep shade as protection from the sun, in the winter you often find deer herded up and bedded down on open and south-facing hillsides. All they need here are a few briars and some brush to break up their outline. Be sure to give these areas close scrutiny.

33

In big woods settings, whitetails seek protection from the bitter cold by wintering under the canopy in stands of native evergreens, like hemlock, white pine and mixed spruce/fir. The existence of adequate thermal cover is often crucial to the survival of a wintering northern deer herd. Avoid hunting those areas where loggers have removed the thermal cover, especially after a long hard winter. You may see fewer deer in the vicinity due to high deer mortality.

Glassing gives you good information, no matter what time of year you can get out in the field.

A tree trunk can steady your hand for the shot.

34

Another kind of travel lane is not as easily recognizable, and that is the line that separates one type of cover from another. Bucks weave in and out and along the edge of two species of vegetation as they search for a doe in heat or as they travel from bedding cover to feeding areas. The most valuable of these travel lanes is the crease that separates softwoods and hardwoods in big woods settings.

35

Other travel routes to observe include the invisible line that separates alders and softwoods along the shore of a lake or river, and the easy walking space between mature hardwoods and first/second generation "take-over" saplings on the edges of abandoned farm fields. Of course, the imaginary line that separates patches of sumac, dogwood, goldenrod or choke cherry with an active agricultural field like alfalfa, soybeans or corn are a still-hunter's bread and butter in farm country.

36

Bucks are attracted to bedding areas, food sources and travel routes where natural vegetation covers the terrain features. You'll find the best bedding areas at higher elevations thick with mountain laurel, great feeding locations between a stout beaver dam and an apple orchard. And you'll find the best travel routes combine terrain features that block your forward progress by promoting ankle-twisting undergrowth.

Bucks travel long distances to feed on acorns, passing up other nutritious foods in the process. If you can locate a hidden stand of nut-bearing oaks, your chances of scoring on a racked buck will soar.

Feeding Locations

37

Without a doubt, woodland bucks are attracted to 2- to 7-year-old clear-cuts like their farmland cousins are to alfalfa. Clear-cuts, especially those irregularly shaped with a lot of edge, may offer everything a buck requires. Here is where he finds food, in the form of succulent new growth early in the year and browse once late fall and winter arrives, plus cover, in the form of ½-inch to 3-inch (1.25 to 7.5 cm) saplings and replanted softwoods. If there is water and an ample resident doe population, a buck really has little need to venture out of the clear-cut!

Over the years I have killed two of my heaviest bucks in or near clear-cuts, a 6-point sans brow tines that dressed out at 200 pounds (90 kg) even, and a 10-point that tipped the scales at 220 pounds (99 kg).

38

Stands of oak are a food source that attracts bucks with wild abandon. Indeed, when available, acorns are a whitetail's first food choice, with about a dozen preferred varieties distributed throughout their range. Beechnuts and hickory nuts are also an important mast crop to pay close attention to.

39

Apples are the third concentrated food source deer can't seem to get enough of. Fortunately, old orchards are as easy as clear-cuts to locate. Simply examine your topo map for those rows of irregular green circles indicating an orchard, or you can hike through abandoned farmland. It seems every old farm had a crab apple tree or two in the backyard. I've never found an apple tree that didn't eventually have deer nosing around under its branches come deer season.

SECRET BUCK HIDEOUTS

I was stunned. We had been snow-tracking a buck's trail, three hunters abreast, since first light and had not yet seen hide or hair of him. The big woods buck led us through thick swamps and hilltops choked with mountain laurel, but he was on a mission it seemed and never slowed down or gave us a chance to get close. Suddenly the trail took an abrupt right turn and passed in front of me. I looked over at my father to see if the buck track at my feet was made by the same buck we had been trailing for almost two hours. He motioned with his hand that it was and for me to be silent.

I turned in the direction the buck took and stepped forward with my Model 12 at port arms. Without warning, the racked buck exploded from the tangled branches of a blow-down a mere 25 yards (23 m) away and high-tailed it across a nearby creek and up an open hillside like a bunny kicked from a brush pile. I was mesmerized by his sleek form and white rack, and although at that distance it should have been an easy shot, I missed him clean.

That day is etched in my memory for a couple of reasons. One, even if you have a safe shot at an escaping buck, the odds are with the buck. And two, bucks hide in the oddest locations, places the average hunter would overlook. Here are some not-so-obvious hot spots where wise bucks hide during daylight hours.

Natural Camouflage

40

Blow-downs attract bucks for a variety of reasons. The crisscrossed branches and dead leaves offer a resting buck ample cover, but just as important they allow the buck to twist his head and neck to see all around without divulging his whereabouts. In this manner, a buck can observe you as you approach and gauge whether you see him or are going to pass by without noticing his huddled form.

Try this exercise, and I think you will see what I mean. During the post-season, follow a set of buck tracks in the snow. Without fail, you'll find that he will turn and investigate, at least from a distance, any thick blow-downs he encounters. That's because other deer, does too, often bed inside.

Bucks bed down in blow-downs because they offer concealment and a wide range of vision. They are also good places to wait for a buck to pass by.

41

Abandoned farm fields are soon taken over by goldenrod, briars, Queen Anne's lace and tall grasses. These are often the last place anyone looks for bedded deer simply because there doesn't seem to be enough cover to hide a mouse, much less a buck.

Surprisingly, in such a setting bucks often let you approach quite closely before they high-tail it to the nearest stand of cover. One season while still-hunting along the edge of a goldenrod field my eyes were constantly drawn to a "funny looking thing" some 40 yards (37 m) away. I stopped often to glass the adjacent wood lot, but my neck kept craning back to the open goldenrod field. Finally, I glassed the funny looking thing and was caught off guard. It was a bedded buck looking right at me, his black nose and white rings around his eyes sticking out like some Halloween costume. That buck must have figured out I had him pegged because before I could even think about taking a shot he stood up and bounded away.

42

In the Northeast, a patch of mountain laurel is always a solid bet for a big buck hideaway.

Bucks bed in open sunny areas inside the patch as well as along rocky ledges and anywhere along the edge where they can face into the wind. The tangle of twisted and low-hanging branches allows bedded bucks to easily detect our approach and skulk off before we are even remotely aware of their presence.

How do you know a buck is holed up inside a patch of laurel? In the winter, a set of tracks leading into a likely patch and not exiting is the best clue, aside from an actual sighting. In the absence of snow, large tracks, large-diameter droppings, thick rubs and wide oval beds signal that bucks have been hanging in and around the patch, and if deer sightings have been sparse, you can bet more than one buck is hiding out in the laurel.

Still-hunting through a patch of laurel is rarely an option. Instead, post along a downwind or crosswind edge, and wait for a buck to saunter into view. Rut-specific calling and rattling are also options. Even in those areas where drives are possible, bucks often circle around or just hold tight and let the drivers pass. When threatened, deer won't leave the safety afforded by a thick patch of mountain laurel!

43

One of the most unlikely sites of refuge for a racked buck is a single tree, the kind that is plain to see for miles (kilometers) around. It doesn't seem to matter if the tree is on the open prairie or inside an expansive uncut corn lot, bucks will bed nearby.

Why? Although that tree, no matter how insignificant in size, helps to break up their outline, I think the main draw is that the tree serves as a navigational landmark.

EVEN SMALL SPACES HOLD BIG DEER

One season in New York I spied a 20-square-yard (16.8 sq m) stand of trees and brush centered between four plowed cornfields. There wasn't another piece of cover for over 1 mile (1.6 km). On a hunch I walked across the field to the trees and brush, but as I neared I realized that any deer bedded there could certainly see me and would make a run for it before I ever got within shotgun range.

Well, I was right. Before I could get too close, twenty-some deer—including two bucks—erupted from the brush lot and struck out across the adjacent fields without ever giving me an opportunity for a shot. I figured the best way to hunt this hot spot was to be in place before shooting light and hope a buck shows up after things settle down.

In similar fashion, small patches of cover also hide deer on the open prairie. One season I watched a buck sneak out of a stand of sweet clover just after legal shooting light. I returned the next morning hoping he would try to sneak back in, but after four hours nothing showed up. I decided to perform a one-man push through the 40-foot (12 m) swatch of chest-high clover. Much to my surprise, as I neared the end with only a few feet (meters) of cover left, I actually felt a buck stand up and bolt across the open ground. I almost stepped on him! Unfortunately the huge drop-tined buck escaped unscathed, and I never did see him again.

I don't know what the attraction is, but bucks' lairs are routinely found around stone walls.

Bucks in the Midwest, Deep South and Northeast also seek out abandoned machinery for bedding sites, and are often found inside thick stands of brush and briars.

It doesn't take much cover to hide a buck. In fact, about 5 square feet (0.45 sq m) of tall grass is all it takes, and when bucks are under pressure they seek out these out-of-the-way strongholds humans often ignore.

Man-Made Camouflage

45

Stone walls are most common east of the Mississippi where rocky farmland prevails. Early farmers cleared the fields and piled the rocks in long lines as much as a means of disposal as anything else.

Bucks often bed along stone walls, especially the corners, because they offer some protection from the elements as well as the prying eyes of a predator. But the main reason bucks find stone walls such appealing bedding areas is the simple fact that deer of both sexes use stone walls as conduits or guides as they travel about their turf. Indeed, bucks and does often walk parallel to a stone wall, crossing back and forth at natural breaks in the stonework. The best places are near known crossings. Look for faint trails as well as rubs, scat and beds to confirm usage.

46

Years ago in Montana I jumped a racked buck that had bedded down next to an old combine. I was surprised he was there, but after looking back at the event, I realized the odd piece of farm machinery was really the only cover available on an otherwise stark and flat landscape.

47

Bucks are very sensitive to human intrusion and adjust their daily routines to avoid human contact. Sometimes bucks go nocturnal; sometimes they avoid danger by getting as far away from humans as possible.

48

During the rut, bucks bed near stone walls so they can keep tabs on the local doe traffic. The trick is to first expect a buck to be bedded with his back up against the wall and, second, to look for a bedded buck versus a standing buck as you creep along.

49

I don't know what the attraction is to old hay balers, wood-railed wagons and rusting plows, harrows and rakers, but bucks often bed alongside them.

The best way to hunt these old pieces of junk is to first work your way crosswind and into gun range. Then glass the surrounding terrain carefully for that telltale flicker of an ear or antler tip. If nothing moves, try a buck grunt or doe bleat.

50

One of the safest places for a big buck during the deer season is on the median between two interstate highways. Although traffic noises interfere with their hearing, they don't seem to mind as long as humans don't stop and exit their vehicles.

Once in a while bucks cozy right up to humans to bed where they least expect it—in the backyard.

THE OLD CELLAR HOLE

A buck's attraction to cellar holes is in part due to the presence of an old farmstead. Often there are apple trees nearby and an old mowing or two that has long since reverted to a meadow. The bucks are understandably bedding close to preferred food sources. The best cellar holes seem to have topographical features that funnel deer into the area, such as creek beds or gentle slopes, and it is these that deserve extra attention.

You can certainly sneak to old cellar holes, but some of my friends relish carting a folding chair with them and then sitting inside the cellar hole all day waiting for a buck to come in and bed down. You must approach with caution, being careful not to disturb any nearby bucks patrolling the area in the dark, and then be in position before shooting light.

THE PERFECT TREE STAND

There is no doubt about it: Hunting whitetails from an elevated platform is a killer technique! Position a tree stand correctly, and you should easily avoid a buck's sharp eyes, rotating ears and uncanny sniffer long enough to take him with one well-aimed shot. This does not mean, however, that any stand site will work for you. Some set-ups are simply better than others.

You can easily ruin a good stand by trimming too much. Remember, bucks are often attracted to a certain location because of its dense cover. Trim too much away and the buck simply picks a different travel route.

51

Erect your tree stand only after carefully considering a host of factors, including food preferences, weather conditions, hunting pressure and stage of the rut. Don't set up a stand based on last year's scouting information. A lot could have happened in the interim. Crop rotation, a poor mast crop, new housing projects and logging operations, for example, can all impact a deer's daily routine and cause him to abandon last year's hot spot.

52

Be sure your stand is well concealed. If it is visible from the ground, it should look like part of the forest and nothing more. If you must trim branches around the stand, do so sparingly and only enough to come to full draw without interference. Just remember that the branches you cut away are the same branches that afford you cover.

The same goes for shooting lanes. Keep in mind that mature bucks do not like to stick their necks out. Wide open shooting lanes spell d-a-n-g-e-r to an alert buck and are subsequently avoided. Besides, the brush you cut down and remove is often the very same cover that attracts local bucks!

53

The perfect tree stand is one you erected, fair, square and legal. Never hunt from a stranger's tree stand. Not only is it unethical, but it may be defective or not have been set up correctly, which in some cases could be an accident waiting to happen.

54

Position your tree stand no higher than necessary. In some cases, a 10-foot (3 m) perch is more than high enough, whereas in other situations a stand 15 to 20 feet (4.5 to 6 m) up is required. Keep in mind that the higher you go, the more acute the shot angle becomes on nearby deer.

Hunting from a stand in late season has its own set of problems. There is less cover and those few bucks that somehow survived the fall fusillade are on high alert. You can overcome some of these obstacles by placing your tree stand a few feet (meters) higher than usual and positioning it so that you take your shot sitting down after the buck passes by. A quartering-away shot is the best angle for a nervous buck.

55

The best strategy is to have a tree stand that allows you to approach the site and then climb on board without alerting any deer to your presence. You can start as soon as you park your vehicle by remaining quiet as you assemble your gear. Do not talk, slam doors or wave flashlights about.

Check the wind and then choose the route with the most privacy. You do not want your scent drifting into suspected bedding grounds or preferred feeding areas, for example, nor do you want deer to see you crossing open fields or gas line rights-of-way either. You especially don't want to cross any hot buck trails.

Finally, use a fawn bleat to calm down any nearby deer once you are settled in.

56

The perfect tree stand is one only you and a close friend know about. Don't brag about the bucks you are seeing on Farmer Brown's farm and don't give away the stand's exact whereabouts. Tell the boys at the archery shop you have a stand in the old apple orchard, and sooner or later one of those guys will be setting up nearby—legally or otherwise.

Even if you are tight-lipped about your hunting turf, don't park near your hunting grounds or an obvious trail head. Instead, leave your vehicle some distance away to help confuse trespassers and claim jumpers about the specific location of your tree stand.

57

You should be able to stay aloft all morning or all afternoon if necessary. Start by choosing a stand design that allows you to sit still without fidgeting. A seat that is too high, too low or too small can cramp your leg muscles, forcing you to stand and stretch; so can a stand that is not positioned correctly. If the stand is tilted, for example, it will throw your weight off balance, as will a knot in the trunk pressing against your back. Even facing a rising or setting sun can raise havoc on your ability to remain motionless during prime time.

Nothing ruins a hot spot faster than human stench. Practice staying as scent-free as possible.

58

Be sure your stand is clean and free of human odors. This means you are careful in your approach and exit routines, and you do not wander around the area looking for deer sign or pacing off shooting distances. Use a range finder and write down the distance to various objects for future reference. Tape them to the inside of your riser if need be.

Some hunters go so far as to spray scent eliminators on anything they touch or rub up against, including tree steps, pull-up ropes and the tree itself. You can never be too careful in this regard.

59

Have a second or even third stand in position to take advantage of major changes in wind direction brought about by storms and other varying weather conditions.

Don't be tempted to sit in your favorite tree stand if the wind is blowing your scent in the direction you expect a buck to come from. Once a mature buck knows you are lurking nearby, he will undoubtedly avoid the area for several days—or even the rest of the season.

60

Don't hunt the same stand on a daily basis. Ideally, you would hunt from that stand only once, taking one well-aimed shot at a buck before you climb down from your first time on board. Otherwise, any more than three times a week would be excessive.

The only exception is during the peak of the rut when bucks from near and far are pursuing does 24/7. Those stands that are set up along natural funnels can be bowhunted almost daily now.

61

Position your tree stand in a clump of trees whenever possible, as opposed to a single tree with no branches. If you are unsure if you are silhouetted or not, view the stand from a deer's perspective and then make adjustments as necessary.

Hunt a stand only on the rarest of occasions when all conditions are ideal. It's your best chance to bag a nice one, like this buck.

EXIT STRATEGY

Get out of your tree stand quickly and quietly, avoiding all metal clanging. In case an unscrupulous hunter does find your stand, undo the lower set(s) of steps and hide them nearby. He may have found your secret stand site, but it is unlikely he will be able to hunt from it—at least on the day he finds it!

Next, choose an exit route that will help you avoid contact with any deer. Keep in mind that getting to your stand quietly is much easier in broad daylight than when it's dark. Can you sneak out without making a racket or disturbing nearby deer? After a morning hunt, for example, you can cross most openings with impunity, but in the evening you would need to avoid meadows and other feeding areas, even if it means taking the long way around.

And don't walk out too quickly or in a forthright manner. As with your approach, you must "bob and weave," avoiding known trails and probable concentrations of deer. Sneak out! And when you get to your vehicle, don't talk, turn on the radio or bang gear around. Deer study your exit strategy as quickly as they study your approach.

Is the perfect tree stand a portable or a permanent set-up? Permanent stands have three built-in problems: One, as soon as a buck picks you off, he'll give your set-up a wide berth whenever he passes nearby, making the life span of that stand rather short.

Two, permanent stand positions are difficult to fine-tune. You may be in the right church, so to speak, but the wrong pew—you can't move the 5 or 10 yards (4.5 or 9 m) needed to get a killer shot.

Three, moving about as the season unfolds is also impossible with a permanent stand. For instance, keying in on food sources in the early season, such as alfalfa, corn, beans, peas and buckwheat, is generally a good strategy, but sometimes conditions change. A good windstorm, for example, can shake the season's first acorns loose, luring local bucks away from agricultural crops and into the swamp bottoms and steep hardwood ridges to feed on the fallen mast. How are you going to take advantage of this situation if you're relying on permanent stands built during the off-season?

For even better camouflage of your stand, weave a few dead branches into the stand's frame. You want your stand to remain hidden from deer and human eyes.

When you step off the stand, push the main platform up against the tree trunk to reduce its silhouette.

TREE STAND TIPS FOR BOWHUNTERS

There are plenty of reasons a trophy buck is North America's number one big game animal. A mature specimen is sleek, quick afoot and, above all, especially wary. And those antlers! Hardly a serious deer hunter in the woods these days doesn't appreciate a wide-racked buck trotting into view.

Indeed, if it weren't for whitetails, surely there would be far less outdoor industry in North America. Firearms, bows and arrows, camouflage clothing, hunting videos/magazines and a truckload of "must have" accessories all depend on the deer-hunting public to remain in business.

But if you're an avid bowhunter, there is only one accessory that consistently and successfully combats a buck's primary senses. A quality tree stand positioned properly can put you within bow range of one big buck after another, season after season. The key words here are "positioned properly."

64

To help combat a buck's incredible eyesight and ability to notice small changes in his environment, smart bowhunters camouflage their tree stands. No matter what style or model you choose, and no matter how old or new your stand, add a little contrast to your set-up. For example, don't be afraid to spray paint platforms, braces, chains and other hardware, including ladders and climbing pegs. A dab or two of earth-tone color(s) can work wonders in helping you and your stand blend in with your immediate surroundings.

65

Erect your stand in the backyard and, using all your hunting gear, practice getting in and out of your stand before the season opens. Even if you've been bowhunting for several seasons, you'd be surprised what basics you might overlook after a year's absence from the field, like a pull-up rope, a bow hanger, a urine bottle or a grunt tube. Be prepared!

Make practice sessions as realistic as possible. A dry run will help iron out any kinks you might have acquired before the moment of truth arrives.

66

To add more realism, use a lifelike deer target such as the GlenDel Buck from Field Logic. Positioning the deer at various angles helps you better visualize the path of the arrow when it enters the deer's body. In other words, it will teach you the proper aiming point on a buck that is quartering away from you. And it will teach you that aiming behind the shoulder on a quartering-to buck generally results in a gut-shot animal.

67

To sweeten your odds of success over the entire season, learn to make every hunt your "first" by moving your ambush sites according to the vagaries of the rut. Key in on food sources during the early season, fresh rut sign during the pre-rut, and on doe feeding grounds, bedding areas and trails that connect one bedding area preferred by family groups of does and fawns with another during the peak of the rut.

68

It may be illegal in your area to use screw-in steps on public land, and many private landowners do not want them used on their trees, either. When asking permission to hunt private property, tell the landowner you use climbing poles, ladders or steps that fasten to the tree with rope in lieu of screw-in steps. Your chances of gaining access to their land to bowhunt will certainly soar.

69

Practice shooting from your tree stand regularly. Sure, a porch roof or an open second-story window might help, but nothing beats the real thing. You'll not only learn your limitations, but will also find ways to eliminate those unwanted creaks and groans inherent in many metal platforms.

70

Plenty of bucks have been arrowed from bowhunters positioned 10 to 12 feet (3 to 3.6 m) above the ground. Indeed, sometimes all you have to do is get above a buck's normal line of vision to score, especially if you're hunting the thick stuff for bucks. As a rule of thumb, the more open the cover, the higher you must climb to escape detection.

71

To help keep your stand site a secret, leave your vehicle a safe distance from your entry path. Whenever possible, park facing away, on the other side of the road and near the juncture of several private parcels of land. A fence line with posted signs from two or more landowners is always a plus.

72

Know the prevailing winds, and plan several approach routes to your hunting area. You should avoid approaching any stand site from the same direction, to avoid being pegged by local bucks. It only takes two or three trips for these bucks to pick up your routine.

How high to put your stand largely depends on how much background cover you have.

Don't sit in your stand until the season opens—or risk the chance of pushing that buck into another area. Remember, your best opportunity to score is your very first time aloft.

Whether you should take a shot from a sitting or standing position depends on a host of factors, including which direction you expect the buck to approach from.

73

Standing up or sitting down? That's the question most often asked by bowhunters who hunt from an elevated platform. If you position your stand so it faces quartering away from a passing deer, then shooting from a sitting position makes sense. There will be a minimum of movement involved in coming to full draw and you'll have the advantage of broadside or quartering-away penetration. You can also complete the maneuver with a minimum of noise. Sitting does make you handicapped, however, as you can generally only shoot comfortably in a 90-degree arc.

74

View your stand from several different directions, and plug any "holes" that silhouette your position. If need be, weave some of your discarded shooting lane trimmings into a backdrop, or use a commercial skirt to help conceal yourself and your stand.

75

Always leave the seat and platform in the "up" position to further conceal your stand when not in use.

76

Bottlenecks have always been great ambush points, but finding them can be a chore, especially if you are hunting unfamiliar territory. Learn to study topo maps, and these previously unknown ambush points will jump out at you like a flashlight in the dark.

77

After attaching your bow hanger to the tree, practice removing your bow in preparation for a shot. It should be a quiet and smooth maneuver. To avoid any trouble at the moment of truth, you may need to trim a limb or reposition the hanger.

Bucks often use old pastures and grown-over agricultural fields as staging areas—good locations for the careful tree stand hunter.

78

If you're not sure which direction the buck might approach from—as when you are hunting an oak flat or travel lanes during the peak of the rut—then rig your stand so you can shoot standing up. First, position the stand to use the trunk of the tree as a shield to help conceal your silhouette. Then practice coming to full draw from as many angles as possible. You need to know where you can shoot as well as where you cannot before the moment of truth arrives.

79

The juncture of two or more types of cover is generally a good ambush point, especially if there is water nearby. When hunting in the big woods, for example, the invisible line separating a stand of hardwoods from a stand of softwoods is always a hot spot to ambush a rutting buck. A nearby flowing creek or alder swamp is a big plus.

When bowhunting around active agriculture, look for abandoned pastures that border a block of hardwoods as well as several crop fields. Bucks often use the old pasture as a staging area, and are attracted to these sites like moths to a flame. A hedgerow or an irrigation ditch is a definite bonus.

80

A good ambush site can be quickly ruined when you pace off the shooting distance to various landmarks. A palm-sized laser range finder can do the job without spreading your stench about. Be sure you get several measurements, and do so before any deer arrive. A rutting buck can be unpredictable and quickly pass by along unconventional pathways, giving you precious little time to take a reading.

Early-season greenery demands appropriate camo—different from later in the season.

Limbs and branches make just as good camouflage as leaves on a tree.

81

The first rubs of the year are almost always made by the biggest, most dominant bucks of the area, making early-season rub lines a hot stand sight. You must first determine if the buck is running the line in the morning or evening, and then set up accordingly. Indeed, reading buck sign properly as the rut unfolds is often the key to success.

82

Nothing alerts an incoming buck, or another hunter for that matter, to the exact whereabouts of your set-up better than several white spears sticking up from the ground. Use an old trapper's trick and smear dirt and leaves on the stumps of cut saplings to help hide them from prying eyes. Camouflage those shooting lanes!

83

When are portable and climbing tree stands the most dangerous? When you are either getting in or getting out of the stand. Never, for example, step up into your stand. Rather, step down or across to the platform, or in the case of exiting, down or across to a climbing peg or ladder. Always think about safety!

84

Everyone knows it is best to wear a safety belt, but a safety harness is even safer. It is not as likely to tip you upside down or catch you under the ribs should you slip. No matter what style you prefer, keep the line to the tree as short as possible, and don't buy plastic buckles.

85

ATVs have become increasingly popular for getting hunters into the woods and getting tagged game back to camp. Unfortunately, the machines are noisy, and local bucks take heed and quickly adjust their routines. Instead, take a tip from Bill Fargasen of SCENTite blinds: Use an electric golf cart whenever possible. They run silently and do not disturb local buck populations.

86

Trim necessary shooting lanes early in the season, and then do so only sparingly. Bucks quickly notice the "chain-saw" method of construction. To help keep your site a secret from both bucks and claim jumpers, pile cut branches and saplings far from your stand.

TREE STAND TIPS FOR FIREARM HUNTERS

It's no secret among bowhunters that tree stands are deadly ambush sites. Ever since the introduction of the portable platform, bowhunter success rates have soared and now firearm hunters are realizing the many advantages of sitting high. Why are stands so effective? Deer like the thick stuff once the gun season gets under way, and the best way to waylay one is to get above the brush where you can see better and shoot down into an unsuspecting animal.

Tree stands help nullify a buck's three primary senses: sight, sound and smell. But there's more to it than simply sliding a tree stand up an old oak in the early-morning darkness, and then tagging a buck at first light. To be successful, you first have to fine-tune your set-up. Here's how.

87

Where should you erect a tree stand to slug a buck? That depends on your pre-season scouting and past hunting experiences, but trails leading to and from feeding areas are good locations for a first-day, first-light stand. Once the season is under way, escape routes such as hedgerows and ridges leading into swamps are better candidates for an airborne ambush. Other good slug-season sites include trails leading into thick cover, such as uncut cornfields, stands of planted pines, steep gullies, overgrown apple orchards and thickets of dogwood, thorn apple and alder. Once you think about it, anywhere you would normally post during the slug season is a good general location for a tree stand.

Success is sweet!

Fooling a Buck's Nose

88

Your first consideration before erecting your portable stand is wind direction. Any tree stand you use during the shotgun season should be set up downwind or crosswind to where you expect a buck to saunter past.

Erect your stands a month before the season opener, and then keep your distance. This helps the area remain scent free and gives the deer time to become accustomed to their presence.

Scout carefully around water.

89

If you hunt hilly terrain, then daily thermals must also be taken into account. Generally winds rise uphill with the rising sun, and rush downhill with the setting sun. Therefore you may have to erect your tree stand uphill of a preferred trail for an early-morning hunt, and downhill of a preferred trail for an evening hunt.

90

You need more than one tree stand location to cover different times of the day and those days when the winds blow erratically. Be conscious of this need whenever you scout. You can never have too many tree stand sites!

91

A buck can be alerted to your presence by simply sniffing the trail you took to your stand. He is so good at it, you may never know he was in the vicinity! Therefore, approach your stand location carefully. Rubber-bottomed boots and a scent pad or drag-along rag dipped in fox or coon urine help keep your human ground scent to a minimum.

92

While it's always best to avoid sending your airborne scent into the area you suspect the buck is located, you must also avoid crossing any trail he may use to walk past your stand.

93

The best gun stands are prepared well before the season opener. If you must trim shooting lanes, do so a month or more before the first day. Not only will your scent be gone by then, but it will give the local herd time to get used to the changes you made in the woods.

Fooling a Buck's Eyes

94

Your first task is to avoid being silhouetted against the skyline. The best tree stands are set up in a copse of trees or against a large enough tree trunk to conceal your torso.

95

The perfect stand allows you to make the perfect shot by raising your gun undetected. Sitting down is your first choice because it requires only a minimum of movement to complete the act. If you must stand to make the shot, then position your stand so you can use the trunk of the tree as a shield.

96

When trimming, leave a branch with its green leaves hanging on the tree near the stand. Later those fluttering brown leaves help hide not only your silhouette, but also those involuntary hand and head movements we all seem to make on stand.

Deer look up; also camouflage the bottom of your stand.

Recoil is generally not a problem for most black powder enthusiasts, unless you are forced to shoot a "super charged" load off-hand. Climb into a tree stand and burn some powder from unorthodox positions before stepping afield—just to be sure.

97

When selecting a site for your stand, consider which trees would serve as the best shield. A mature hemlock or white pine is ideal in this regard, as is a cluster of 10-inch-thick (25 cm) oaks.

98

How high is high enough? That depends. Most hunters climb 10 to 12 feet (3 to 3.6 m), but if you are situated on a hillside, you may need to go higher. A buck going downhill will be eye level with your position if you don't pay heed.

99

It is also wise at times to wear gloves and a face mask, and/or paint all exposed skin, including face, neck and ears with camo cream. Why? Exposed skin attracts a buck's attention like a moth to a bright campfire, especially when you move your head to see what that crunch, crunch, crunch is off to your left!

100

To help keep a nearby buck from looking up, locate your stand so the buck's attention is riveted on or near the ground when it comes time to take the shot. Set up near a rub, on the inside curve of a bend in the trail, near a stream crossing or close to a natural obstacle in the trail such as a log or a pile of brush. If you can't find such a crossing or natural obstacle, set out a decoy deer, a canister of doe urine or a mock scrape near your stand; they, too, can help you when the moment of truth arrives by keeping the buck's attention at ground level.

Fooling a Buck's Ears

101

Have all cables, wires and harnesses greased, oiled or wrapped in electrician's tape to dampen the squeaks and creaks common to all stands with moving parts. Your neighborhood hardware store may be able to help you with some "liquid rubber" for those troublesome chains.

102

Be sure to dampen the base of the stand. Sometimes just dragging your boot across the base as you turn to shoot can alert a buck to your intentions. Most carpet stores sell indoor/outdoor samples or remnants that are ideal for this project. Make sure they are securely fastened to the stand and that they are not slippery when wet.

103

If your stand is difficult to approach quietly, it's never a bad idea to clear a path and mark the trail with some form of fluorescent markers. Even then, you should plan on being on stand for an hour or so before shooting hours.

104

Once your stand is secured on-site, test it for squeaks and groans by moving all about the platform. (Be sure to wear a safety belt!) Then remove any shards of bark that may come in contact with your body and any branches that might interfere with the swinging of your rifle or shotgun. Even a small dead twig can spoil a hunt if it rubs up against your shotgun's barrel.

Use the "stop-n-go" approach to reach your tree stand site. Bucks instinctively recognize the steady cadence of human movement.

Safety First

105

Keep in mind that tree stands can be quite dangerous. Always climb using the three-point system—only one hand or foot away from the tree at a time. This way, if you slip, you will be able to catch yourself before falling to the ground.

106

Make a habit of checking your stand carefully for vandalism and booby traps before climbing on board. A hunting partner returned to her stand after the morning hunt only to find the stand had been tampered with and the padlock cut away. She realized the damage only after the platform collapsed under her weight, tossing her to the ground. Fortunately, she was not seriously hurt.

107

Once you're belted in, be sure to secure all your gear. I had a hand climber come loose in the wind and knock me silly one morning. Now I tie it down with a couple of bungee cords.

108

After a fall, always unload your gun and check the barrel for any kind of obstructions.

109

Never raise or lower a loaded firearm. If you drop it, it's apt to send a slug through the bottom of your tree stand.

110

Before you climb on board, examine your stand for unusual stress or damage, especially in the dark. I once had a porcupine chew my platform up so badly I had to bring it home to be repaired.

111

Remember to brush off the snow so you don't slip once you're in the stand.

112

If you wear camo, also wear fluorescent orange even if your state or province doesn't mandate it. At least hang an orange vest from a nearby branch. Not only can it protect you from being mistaken for game and other shooting accidents, studies have shown that other hunters avoid hunting areas whenever they see someone already there in orange. And that means you'll keep your hot spot all to yourself.

Test your ability to shoot in various directions.

Some sort of pull-up rope is a small investment for safety.

ALWAYS THINK SAFETY

Tree stands must be safe to use. Stands that have been left outdoors all season long need to be inspected carefully for splits and cracks before you ever step on board again. Extreme weather, claim jumpers, saboteurs, animal right's advocates and others can all raise havoc with any hunting property left unattended in the woods.

Even if you remove your stands at the end of each season, field test each one before the next opener. If you have any reservations about its safety or effectiveness, get rid of it and purchase a new one. Your life and well-being are worth a lot more than any whitetail.

What is the most dangerous tree stand in the woods? The one that is handmade from leftover lumber. Rain, sun and especially wind can weaken the wood and even pull nails and screws from support beams, causing it to collapse when you set your weight down. Never trust them!

SCENT CONTROL

Of a buck's three primary senses, there is no doubt that his sniffer is the most powerful. When an unsuspecting buck sees something out of place or hears an unusual sound, he will most likely investigate the commotion from a safe distance before skulking back into the shadows. But let him get a fresh whiff of his age-old enemy—man—and he could disappear from your life forever, or at least until the end of the season.

American Indians used sweat lodges and then kept an eye on the wind to minimize their odors. Modern man has other tricks at his disposal to keep human fragrances from drifting into a buck's nostrils.

113

When it's time to go hunting, take a shower with a scent-free soap, and don't put on any outer clothing until you reach your hunting area. Of course, this is easier said than done when temperatures are in the single digits.

114

Hunting boots stink! To eliminate unwanted odors, spray the inside with a good over-the-counter foot powder, and then store them in a clear, scent-free plastic bag until it's time to go hunting. Do not wear your boots while pumping gas or around camp where they can pick up strange odors.

115

Wash all your hunting clothing with a scent-free detergent and then store them in a scent-free plastic container with leaves, twigs, weeds and dirt from your hunting area. This helps reduce your human odors.

Five minutes of shivering are worth it!

SCENTite Blinds have a 30-foot (9 m) length of plastic pipe that vents warm air and human odors from inside the enclosed blind. I have had bucks walk downwind within a few yards (meters) of the blind and not get even a whiff of me inside.

Decoys need the scent-eliminator treatment, too.

116

Consider hanging your outer hunting clothing, including your charcoal scent-blocker suit, in a barn with farm animals. Area deer are already used to the strong smell of animal manure.

117

Get rid of your old hats! They soak up human odors like a sponge. Spray a new hat with a good scent eliminator, and then only wear it in the field. Change hats at least once a week.

118

You can spray scent eliminators on insulated Gore-Tex boots with good results.

119

Spray a quality scent eliminator on your bow, quiver and arrows, and allow them all to dry before stepping afield. Do the same with your firearm. Reapply every few hours when on stand.

120

When handling buck lures, urines, attractant scents, decoys or climbing pegs, be aware that deer will walk right up and smell the canisters, the imitation deer and metal steps without hesitation. Always wear rubber gloves, gloves sprayed with scent eliminators or charcoal-activated gloves to avoid leaving a human odor.

Bowhunters beware! A buck can detect your entrance and exit trails even in the snow!

121

Don't put any scents or lures on your clothing or place them directly upwind from your stand. A buck might be enticed by a doe estrous concoction, for example, but if he also smells you, he will immediately exit the scene. It's better to place a buck lure or attractant scent 20 yards (18 m) or so off to the side. Hopefully a buck will walk into the scent stream before he picks up your odor and saunters upwind past your stand, offering you an easy broadside opportunity.

122

Be more concerned with the human scent you leave on the ground than with airborne human stench. The latter dissipates rather quickly into the wind, but ground scent can linger for hours, spooking deer long after you've gone home and to bed.

Deer play the wind too.

123

To keep ground scent to a minimum, be careful where you walk and what you touch, and avoid rubbing up against any waist-high weeds or underbrush. Rubber-bottomed boots sprayed liberally with a good scent eliminator can help, as can foot pads and drag rags soaked in fox, skunk, raccoon or coyote urine.

124

There is no cover-up scent that can handle human odors 24/7. Even Native Americans played the wind after spending hours in the sweat lodge. You should do the same.

125

Run out of scent eliminator spray? When in a pinch, store your hunting clothing in a perfume-free plastic bag stuffed with dirt, dead leaves and other forest debris overnight. It won't kill all the human odor, but it could reduce it substantially.

TRAIL CAMERAS

Deer hunters have always longed for gadgets that can enhance the outdoor experience—and increase success rates on trophy bucks. Portable tree stands immediately come to mind along with the compound bow, replaceable blade broadheads, camouflage, range finders, fiber-optic sighting systems, special deer lures and variable grunt tubes. And this is just a partial list!

In recent years, few items have ignited the imagination of deer hunters more enthusiastically than the use of trail cameras as a tool for both deer hunting and deer management.

Indeed, a friend set up his trail cam along the edge of an open hay lot one recent summer evening and then stood on a nearby hillside to watch the action. His trail cam soon "flashed" a nighttime deer, but then much to his surprise he witnessed five more "flashes" in the same field. In 10 minutes, that buck tripped a half-dozen trail cameras belonging to other deer hunters!

Today's trail cameras range widely in price. Some are film loaded, others are digital and decked out with motion detectors, heat sensors and enough mega pixels to get your big-buck photos published in any quality magazine.

126

Sometimes you can discover a buck's core area by setting up trail cameras along travel corridors that lead to and from known food sources as well as over the food source itself. You can start in early spring and continue on through the summer. By early fall many bucks are still holding summer feeding patterns, important information for the season opener.

127

One strategy is to set up your camera over a food plot close to a high-traffic area like an entrance trail. Put it 36 inches (91 cm) off the ground and, if possible, facing north.

A trail camera set up along the edge of a feeding area might help you discover previously unknown deer, such as those bucks that have long gone nocturnal.

Deer hair caught on a barbed-wire fence only tells you a deer crossed at that point. It doesn't tell you when the deer crossed or the sex or age of the deer. A trail camera, however, can often give you that information—even when it's raining or snowing.

128

Where else can you hide a trail camera? The options are almost endless: near natural food sources, staging areas, along the periphery of hot bedding sites and along high-traffic areas such as funnels, fence lines and edges of ravines and swamps.

129

Limiting your camera checks to once a week will keep human scent to a minimum. It also lessens the chances of spooking bucks to the next farm or causing them to go nocturnal.

130

From mid to late fall, set up trail cams along scrape lines and rub lines to learn which trails mature bucks are actually using and which funnels they prefer to pass through. This helps with day-to-day stand placement.

131

Do not aim the camera into direct sunlight, as images will appear washed out. A poorly positioned flash will also produce low-quality photos. Experiment with the angle before you leave it out in the field.

132

Your best opportunity to get high-quality photos of big bucks is during the heat of the rut. But this is the time you should be in the woods hunting and not checking trail cams. You can do both if you set up a camera overlooking a scrape recently freshened by a buck, or a food plot frequented by family groups of does and fawns. Just be aware that the flash may or may not run off the buck.

Trail camera shots can indicate the quality of deer in a herd.

133

Another no-no is to purchase a trail cam with only motion-sensitive detectors. Without a heat sensor, a moving branch triggers the camera, and if you're using film or even a large-capacity flash card, it could fill up quickly with useless photos.

134

With trail cams, a big mistake is to use cheap batteries. It requires a lot of energy to run any trail cam, so purchase the best alkaline or rechargeable batteries you can find. Most should last up to 30 days, depending on air temperature and other weather conditions.

135

Limit the amount of vegetation near the camera lens. When using a flash, the resulting photos often wash out if the vegetation is too heavy.

136

A trail cam can also be used to assess your deer management program. During the off-season, deer return to a food source as long as they aren't pressured. Thus a trail cam set up over a supplemental feeder can help you determine what options to consider for better management.

137

From late fall through the winter months, return to filming around food sources. As normal food sources get covered in deep snows, switch to alternate food sources such as clear-cuts and cedar swamps. Your main goal now is to see which mature bucks survived the hunting season and where they spend the winter.

KEEPING DEER FROM PEGGING YOU

It doesn't take long for a buck to figure out what you are up to. In fact, all it takes is for you to spend a few thoughtless days in his bailiwick, and he will learn more about you than you will ever learn about him. He will for example know within three days what you eat, how bad your breath is, what you smell like, what you look like and—if he is really smart—he will even recognize you from afar by your gait.

He will know where your stands are located, where your trail cameras are hidden, and the pathway you take to and from each one. He will know where you park your vehicle, when you arrive and also what time you go home. This knowledge will soon allow him to side-step your every move, avoid every ambush and generally make a fool out of you.

All is not lost, however. Here's how to keep him guessing about your presence long enough to get a shot.

138

The most obvious way bucks learn of our presence is by seeing us skulking about in the field. Not just walking about like a farmer or woodcutter mind you, but sneaking around looking for deer and deer sign. Most of the time we do not see these resident bucks, but they see us—and they know instinctively what we are up to by correctly "reading" our body language. Walk about casually as if you do not have a care in the world, and the deer are not as likely to see you as a predator on the prowl.

139

Do plenty of post season and summer scouting to learn where deer congregate, and then stay out of sight those last few weeks until the season opens. Bedding areas, for example, are best located during your post season scouting trips from the dead of winter right through spring green-up.

140

Learn to be sneaky without putting undue pressure on local deer populations. Your goal is to hunt undisturbed bucks whenever possible.

141

Finish off your pre-season scouting a few weeks before the season opener with a quality pair of binoculars rather than shoe leather. You want to be able to watch bucks moving about unobtrusively, but you want to do so by positioning yourself as far away as possible.

142

Avoid passing close to known concentrations of deer on the way to your hunting site. Steer clear of bedding sites, for example, and don't skirt too close to an opening when deer may be present. A buck is not likely to show himself during daylight hours if he has even the slightest inkling a human being is sneaking about.

Not seeing any bucks? Blame yourself if you are over-hunting the area.

143

Minimize your entrance/exit pattern by not overhunting your tree stand. Once or twice a week is generally ideal; you are courting disaster if you visit the site on a daily basis. Even so, choose alternate routes to your stand when possible.

144

Make sure your rattling and calling sequences are rut specific. An estrous doe bleat or a tending buck grunt in the early season is a sure tip-off to any nearby bucks that something is amiss.

145

Wearing knee-high rubber boots and staying downwind of bedding areas, feeding sites and preferred travel routes while scouting certainly help keep your presence a secret to the local deer herd. So does keeping your body, clothing and all equipment clean and as free of human scent as possible once the season opens. And there's no use bowhunting a hot spot, no matter how clean you are, if the wind is not in your favor, either.

146

Always wear full camo during your pre-season scouting. Even so, don't walk brazenly through transitional cover such as overgrown fields or power line right-of-ways late in the evening when bucks may be crossing.

147

Don't rush to your hot spot. Trophy bucks are often pegged by hunters who sneak-and-peek to their tree stand or ground blind.

In a pinch, you can always use dirt for face camo.

ATVs are a great mode of transport, but should be used sparingly, especially if they are noisy.

148

Be careful where you walk and what you brush up against whenever you are in deer country! Don't, for example, walk on deer trails or through known travel corridors, don't lean up against tree trunks and avoid taking the same scouting routes. And for heaven's sake don't walk back and forth through staging areas, feeding areas and bedding areas looking for deer and deer sign. You are just asking for trouble!

149

Deer have excellent hearing and do not let the snap of a twig or the twang of a barbed-wire fence go unnoticed. You might get away with either sound once, but rarely more than that.

150

Always tuck your pants into your boots, and if foxes, coyotes or raccoons are plentiful in your area, douse those boots and a cotton glove with their urine. This will reduce, but not eliminate, the amount of human odor you leave behind.

151

Getting close to a buck from ground zero is what it's all about. In fact, it's the only way you're going to realistically get a shot. Your goal is to work yourself into position so close to an unsuspecting buck that you can feel his heat. That's when time seems to stand still for a moment or two as you meticulously prepare yourself for the upcoming shot.

152

If you are jumping bucks during your pre-season scouting missions, you are educating these local deer to your predatory intentions.

153

A pattern of noise may lead a buck to avoid a certain area. Consistently parking your vehicle within earshot of your tree stand, for example, causes a buck to shy away just as quickly as the "clang-clank-clang" we get when raising and lowering our archery tackle from the same stand.

Foggy conditions can help you control your scent; the air is heavy and not swirling.

154

Make every effort to be quiet whenever you approach your hunting grounds. Don't drive up to the same parking area day in and day out with the radio blaring, and don't slam the doors. And, above all, don't talk to your hunting partner in loud tones.

155

The steady cadence of a deer hunter walking purposely to his stand—steps that are equal in distance and unidirectional in nature—are as good a warning to a racked deer as the howling of a pack of dogs. Switch to a stop-and-go rhythm that does not alarm deer or other wildlife instead.

156

Deer have excellent hearing, and do not let a snapped twig or the "twang" of a barbed-wire fence go unnoticed. They don't have to see you or smell you to know you are up to no good.

157

Don't scout uncut corn lots, acorn flats or secluded apple orchards when deer are likely to be feeding. Instead, get into the habit of checking out transitional cover and feeding areas during the middle of the day when deer are not likely to be present. And then play it extra safe and stick to the shadows. If you are jumping deer during your pre-season scouting missions, you are educating the local bucks to your predatory intentions.

Chapter 2

STRATEGIES

As the early season comes to a close, successful deer hunters begin to look for those subtle changes that indicate the rut is about to unfold. Bucks' necks begin to swell, for example, and fresh rubs and scrapes can be spotted dotting the landscape. Various new calling strategies can now be employed and those secret buck trails we all know exist can finally be unraveled.

Perhaps most importantly, however, is the need to be a dead shot with your weapon of choice. Generally you only get one crack at a racked buck before he disappears from your life forever. You want to make sure that when that opportunity presents itself, you and your equipment are up to the task.

THE PRE-RUT

The pre-rut is a magical time of year. One day the woods are void of buck sign, and then, seemingly overnight, scrapes and scrape lines, and rubs and rub lines appear in profusion along the edges of swamps, meadows and overgrown logging trails. Bucks are in their prime now and are easily caught flat-footed during daylight hours as they roam about looking for the season's first estrous does.

The onset of the pre-rut heralds a change in deer behavior. It should also signal that it's time to change your hunting strategies. No longer are bucks feeding and bedding where they were all summer long. As the days get shorter, the act of breeding becomes a dominant force in the life of a buck. And it is this sudden urge to breed that makes them so susceptible to the bowhunter.

158

The hallmark of the pre-rut is undoubtedly the sudden appearance of the season's first scrapes. Don't waste your time with those found near feeding areas and around open fields, as they will have been made after sunset. Instead, concentrate your efforts in the thick stuff near suspected buck bedding areas. Keep in mind that early pre-rut bucks are still primarily nocturnal, so you want to stay on stand until the last legal second of shooting light.

159

As the days get shorter, bucks spend more and more time around feeding areas looking for estrous does. And as they do, rubs emerge just within sight and downwind of known doe feeding areas. You must figure out how you can climb on board without contaminating the area with your ground scent. These stands can be successful both in the morning and late afternoon.

The season's first scrapes and scrape lines announce a change in buck behavior. It is time to abandon food sources and key in on fresh rut sign. Still-hunting scrape lines becomes the preferred tactic until all the does are bred. I arrowed this buck as he worked a scrape line while still-hunting during the peak of the rut.

Territoriality

160

The mysterious appearance of fresh rubs and new rub lines is another clue the pre-rut has begun. Look for fresh rubs along trails leading away from morning feeding areas, especially wide open fields frequented by does and fawns. These are easy to spot from a distance, as the shiny side of the rub faces the field. A larger than average set of deer prints should help confirm a mature buck is in the area.

One trick to bowhunting these rubs and rub lines during the early pre-rut is to follow the trail back away from the fields. Then look for a natural funnel such as a brush line, a creek bottom or even a steep ridge, and set up accordingly. A secondary food source, such as a lone apple tree or a grove of acorns, is a plus. You'll have to climb aloft using available starlight, as bucks begin exiting these openings soon after first light.

161

Sometimes one or two buck contact grunts will be enough to bring a racked buck to within bow range. Exit routes, entry routes, scrape lines and rub lines near suspected bedding areas are all good places to call from. For best results, try to match the tone to the age of the deer. For example, if you suspect he is a mature animal, use a deep grunt. Tone it down if you're dealing with a younger buck. After all, you don't want to scare him off; you want him to "think" he's the boss!

162

Bowhunting the pre-rut successfully often means quickly setting up a tree stand for an evening or two in areas you have never hunted before. Don't contaminate this new site with your scent by pacing off various shooting distances from the base of the tree stand. A quality range finder can solve that problem by accurately gauging probable shooting distances from your stand without fouling the site with your human odor.

163

Pre-rut bucks don't always appear in front of your stand according to plan. This is where a drag rag soaked with non-rutting buck urine can be advantageous (estrous doe urine is unnatural at this time of the year and may spook local bucks). Lay down a scent trail in the late afternoon on the downwind side of a buck's suspected bedding or feeding area. Your goal is to spread a urine trail perpendicular to expected deer traffic, not parallel to it. Just be sure not to end the trail at your ambush point or tree stand site or you'll have a hard time getting a shot off. Instead, loop your scent trail around your stand, giving you a better broadside opportunity.

164

Although a buck may be preoccupied with the scent trail, position your tree stand so that you can use the tree's trunk as a shield, and before you climb on board be sure to hang your drag rag along the trail as a "stopper." Hopefully a buck that cuts your scent trail will change direction and follow that trail back to your stand.

WORKING A MOCK SCRAPE

Doctoring a mock scrape or freshening an existing scrape can also tweak a buck's sense of territoriality. Wildlife Research's Ron Bice likes to use a "dripper" to inspire competitive action. The dripper is activated by changes in air temperature that allow it to expel lure only during daylight hours.

"The idea is to position it in an area where a buck passes in the early morning on his way back to his bedding area," says Bice. "If you use a territorial scent, the buck might become conditioned to the scent and hang around a bit during those early-morning hours hoping to intercept the intruder buck.

"Indeed, I've had as many as five bucks work mock scrapes set up in this fashion, each buck returning again and again to add his scent to the scrape much like neighborhood dogs keep urinating on the local fire hydrant in an effort to maintain dominance."

165

Calling can be a very effective technique all during the pre-rut period. But sometimes a buck will "hang up" just out of bow range despite your best efforts. When that happens, Chris Kirby from Quaker Boy gives them the one-two punch. "I like to give an estrous doe bleat three or four times, and watch his reaction," says Kirby. "It tells him there is a doe in the vicinity, and she is in season. If he continues to hold his ground, then I give a second series of estrous doe bleats. If he continues to stand statue-like still, then I grunt at him, softly, three or four times.

"I am trying to create an illusion which in effect tells the buck there is a doe in heat nearby, but an intruder buck has just entered the area, and he is interested in mating with that doe. This combination of calls should be all it takes to get the 'hung up' buck to commit himself."

Scrape Lines

166

Examine the scrape carefully. A buck often rubs his face in the scrape and in so doing leaves impressions of his antlers in the soft earth. If he is a mature buck, you might be able to discern the width of the rack, the number of points, the length of those points and the mass of the two main beams.

Grunt tubes work!

You can learn a lot about a buck by studying scrapes and nearby ancillary sign.

Midday scouting helps you keep tabs on the unfolding rut as well as the whereabouts of doe feeding and bedding areas.

167

You can sometimes predict where a new scrape line will emerge, such as along an old logging road exiting a thick stand of evergreens or near the edge of a small stream. The best way to check on this is through midday scouting. Only now you want to bring a small portable tree stand with you, complete with screw-in steps, in case you have a late-afternoon opportunity!

168

If there are no antler impressions in a scrape, odds are a young buck laid down the scrape line. Look at the overhanging branch to give yourself further evidence. If it is as big as your thumb in diameter and looks as if it were twisted apart by a hay baler, you might still be looking at the "works" of a mature buck.

169

Over the years bowhunting scrape lines has become my favorite pre-rut tactic. Indeed, you can learn a lot about a buck from a series of fresh scrapes. For example, using the surrounding sign, a scrape line can point you to his preferred bedding area as well as his preferred feeding area. It can indicate not only direction of travel and line of travel, but also the probable age of the deer, and the relative weight of his body.

170

When is the best time to set up on a fresh scrape line? Scrape lines are generally hot for 10 to 14 days, but become less important as the rut kicks into high gear, so the best time to hunt a scrape line is as soon as possible!

171

If you prefer to still-hunt during the pre-rut as I do, start each day with a plan based on what you think a buck will be doing on the day you step afield. For example, during the pre-rut, bucks are not bedded down at first light but are spending more and more time after sunrise monitoring local doe populations. A good still-hunting route then would be to start out on the periphery of a known buck bedding area and work slowly toward the closest known doe feeding area. Rely on terrain features such as ridges and ravines as well as edges of cover to help identify the pathway of a morning buck. A few fresh rubs should help keep you on track.

172

The very first day you find scrapes and scrape lines along the edges of fields, rush back into the woods and erect your stand where last season's scrape lines were—even if no new scrape line has yet appeared. If the buck that made last year's scrape line survived, you might just catch him laying down another line of scrapes. And if he didn't survive, another buck might take his place and choose to lay down a series of scrapes for himself. Either way, you only have 2 or 3 days to hunt over one of these early pre-rut scrape lines before it is abandoned for several weeks to the entire season. This brief flurry of activity is often called the early rut.

173

A scrape line can also tell you when that buck is likely to return. Let's say that you find a scrape line just off a heavily used feeding area. After examining the series of scrapes, you determine he worked that scrape line in the wee hours of the morning when he exited the scene because the duff was tossed back toward the feeding area. Add that bit of lore to the large tracks and a couple of nearby 3-inch (7.5 cm) rubs, and you could get a crack at that mature buck at first shooting light.

174

A scrape line coming down off a mountain with the forest duff tossed uphill probably indicates a late-afternoon assault would be best. That is, the buck is working the scrape line in the evening after he leaves his bedding area. On the other hand, if the duff was tossed

downhill, the buck is probably traveling this route on the way back to his bedding area. This would be an excellent late-morning stand. Again, look for beam and tine marks in the scrape for clues as to the size and shape of his rack.

Waning Pre-Rut

175

The best way to get a shot at a buck in his bedding area is to wait for a steady prevailing wind and then sneak in on foot. A stormy day will also work as the moisture and high winds help camouflage your approach. The real secret is to still-hunt with a crosswind and look for him to be bedded down, not standing.

176

You will know when the pre-rut is ending and the rut is about to peak when bucks abandon most active scrapes and scrape lines. This, coupled with regular sightings of racked bucks crossing open grasslands and vacant field lots in the middle of the day, should tell you it is time to once again change your hunting strategies.

177

Your task now is to watch where the does are eating and bedding and which trails they're using to connect the two, without disturbing their daily routines. Indeed, it is time now to stop hunting most rub lines and scrape lines, and begin shadowing the does.

The waning pre-rut is a great time to still-hunt through a buck's bedding area. Play the wind and look for a buck to be on his belly, not standing upright.

178

The late pre-rut may be one of the best times to sneak into a buck's bedroom. Once the rut kicks into high gear, a buck will be going nose to tail with one estrous doe after another, feeding where she feeds and bedding where she beds for up to three days at a time. And when he is done with one he will look for another, rarely visiting his scrapes, scrape lines or preferred bedding area in the process. Thus your chances of tagging him then by setting up nearby his bedding area will be quite poor.

A buck decoy positioned near a bedded doe decoy can sometimes lure a passing buck into bow or gun range.

Stopping Bucks on the Prowl

179

Plan ahead and station a couple of deer decoys. A bedded doe and a standing yearling buck, for example, can give the appearance of an estrous doe being hounded by an amorous buck. That sight alone may be enough to trick a mature buck into throwing his hat in the ring. Be sure to use a quality deodorizer on the decoys before you settle down in your stand.

180

Don't whistle or make a noise in an effort to get a passing buck to stop for a shot because if he stops, he will be on "red" alert.

181

Scrape lines offer killer set-ups during the pre-rut, especially those that emanate from thick bedding cover. Erect your stand downwind or crosswind and as close to the thick stuff as you dare, and then imitate the tending grunts of a rutting buck to bring "your" buck into view before dark.

182

In the late season, position your stand higher off the ground than normal and facing away from incoming deer. Bucks that have been chased and shot at during the firearm season are usually quite jittery and will bolt at the slightest hint of trouble.

Sweet success on this buck—everything worked for me as planned!

183

A quality deer lure can turn a passing deer toward your stand. In the early season, buck urine often tweaks a buck's sense of territoriality, but once scrapes and scrape lines begin appearing, switch to a good estrous doe product. Apply the appropriate scent to a drag rag, and walk a figure-eight pattern using your stand as the center. When complete, use the drag rag as a "stopper" by tying it to a nearby branch.

184

There is nothing more disheartening than watching a rutting trophy buck saunter past your stand just out of range. Since it is unlikely you will ever see that buck again, consider climbing down and giving chase.

185

Never leave your tree stand in the woods during the off-season. Wind and moisture can also wreak havoc on nuts, bolts and chains, and rodents can destroy cloth seats and wooden platforms.

Hunting in Big Woods

186

Watch for open areas inside vast expanses of wilderness. They are often used as breeding areas for mature bucks. One fall I studied aerial photos and located a ½-mile (0.8 km) stretch of old logging road deep in the wilderness. Using my topo map and compass, I found that narrow opening the next day. It was simply littered with scrapes and thigh-size rubs.

I found this Vermont mountaintop clearing nearly 25 years ago by studying a topographical map. It had lots of big-buck sign! Unfortunately, I moved out of the area and have not revisited the site.

ALL FOGGED UP

One November afternoon while hunting a distant valley deep in the Adirondacks, the temperature dropped and a cloud bank rolled in. The fog was so thick I could not see more than 40 yards (36 m) in any direction, and as nightfall approached my visibility dropped to near zero. According to my topo map and compass, I still had a 3-mile (5 km) walk through treacherous terrain to the trail head.

I thought was going to have to spend the night in the woods or at least until the fog lifted to avoid a nasty fall. My spine, pelvis, hip and leg had been ravaged by cancer only a few years earlier and I was still somewhat unsteady on my feet.

Suddenly I remembered the whereabouts of a small stream. It flowed downhill a short distance to a major game trail I had discovered earlier in the week. That game trail eventually crossed a hiking trail and that pathway led to my parked 4x4. I slept in my own bed that night!

Dragging out your buck in big woods can be strenuous. This is when pre-season conditioning can help a lot!

Beaver dams are buck magnets in North America. Look for buck sign atop the dam and along the shores.

187

Hot ambush sites for the peak of the rut include saddles between ridges, gentle slopes leading down to river crossings and the edges of steep ravines. Stay camouflaged, and stay downwind.

188

You can always count on finding deer and deer sign around beaver dams. During the peak of the rut, bucks travel far and wide looking for estrous does; in some cases, bucks travel 20 miles (32 km) or more. Dams then become natural funnels for bucks you never knew existed. Set up on the downwind side of the flow where you have a clear view of the dam. Plan on spending the entire day.

189

There are several online map services now available. Many hunters like the state-by-state coverage of topo maps and aerial photographs offered by Maptech.

190

When pioneering new territory, learn one small section at a time. For example, scout the north side of the creek up to the beaver dam before venturing beyond the dam and into the next valley. Soon you will have command of a large tract of forest, an important asset if you should get turned around during inclement weather.

Like beaver dams, clear-cuts attract mature bucks, like this 170-class 13-pointer I took in Idaho.

191

Hunt 2- to 8-year-old clear-cuts like you would any large field. Pick a high spot that lets you see as much terrain as possible and then fine-tune your position once you can establish preferred crossing points.

192

Use a boat to reach the far side of lakes and ponds, places other hunters cannot normally reach. As hunting pressure mounts, bucks from far and wide will be pushed here, improving your chances of filling your tag.

193

Set up a target range in a gully, much like an archer's 3-D course, including moving targets. Taking shots at unknown distances and from unorthodox angles helps make you a crack shot in the deer woods.

194

The most popular big woods strategy is undoubtedly still-hunting. One of the advantages of this method is that it allows you to scout during the season, helping you pinpoint new food sources, bedding areas and hot rut sign.

195

Whenever you venture into the big woods and unfamiliar territory, even if it's only for a day's hunt, be prepared to spend the night. This means having a pack stuffed with at least a dry set of underwear, flashlight and batteries, small plastic tarp, extra compass, waterproof matches, extra wool hat and wool gloves, candy bars, important medications and a whistle in case you must summon help.

196

Bucks also cross along power lines, gas lines and underground telephone lines. These long, narrow strips of brush and various grasses provide miles and miles (kilometers) of edge, ideal whitetail habitat. Bucks sneak from one side to the other along creek bottoms, ravines and fingers of brush that creep into the open lane. Rubs are a dead give-away of their activity.

197

In the early season, still-hunters do best prowling around food sources, such as acorn hollows, beech ridges and grown-over clear-cuts. Look for fresh tracks and piles of droppings for evidence of recent activity. Early mornings and late evenings are the best times to hunt.

Big woods lean-to's, like this Adirondack version, can be a godsend for those deer hunters who want to spend a couple days chasing wilderness bucks.

198

The best deer hunters I know spend time in the woods scouting for deer and deer sign as well as punching paper at 200 yards (183 m) and beyond. When it comes time to shoot, the more confident you are in your hunting abilities, the less likely you will freeze up at the moment of truth.

199

Rub lines often appear in the same area year after year. It pays to keep tabs on these lines during the rut if they lead to and from concentrations of family groups of does and fawns.

200

Use your binoculars to probe the shadows and edge habitat for unusual shapes and out-of-context colors. It is amazing how well a buck can hide even if he's standing only 50 yards (46 m) away. Keep in mind that his eyes and ears are a lot better than that of humans. If he sees or hears you first, you probably won't see him at all.

201

Learn the big woods strategy of tracking. The easiest way to differentiate a buck track from a doe track is to catch a glimpse of a buck in the snow and then follow him as he is laying down a trail. The more trails you follow—buck and doe— the easier it gets.

Tracking down a mature buck in the snow and taking him with a firearm takes as much woodsmanship as still-hunting trophy bucks with archery tackle.

CALLING STRATEGIES

There are two accessories I always take afield with me: a quality pair of binoculars and a deer call. If I am careful, a single note can lure that buck into bow range as if I possessed a magic flute. Do grunt tubes work all the time? No, but most experts are pleased if they can get one out of ten bucks to respond favorably to their renditions.

Early Season

202

Always have an arrow nocked and ready to go before you start calling to unseen deer. It takes only a second for a buck to step into view, and he will be on high alert leaving you precious little time to prepare for a shot.

203

One of the disappointments to calling whitetails during the early season is the response rate. Bucks are not quite worked up enough to be attracted to an all-out buck fight, nor are they likely to come running to an estrous doe bleat. They investigate a contact grunt from a young buck or doe, or the plaintiff bleat of a fawn. The trick here is to key in on food sources and then set up an ambush in a nearby staging area that offers plenty of cover.

204

Try calling right outside a buck's preferred bedding area late in the morning or an hour or so before darkness. This is risky, but if you're careful it can work on your very first attempt. What call should you use? A couple of moderately toned contact grunts could send that bedded buck into a frenzy. Why? Your rendition might be interpreted as a younger buck invading his territory to look for potential suitors.

205

Yearling buck grunts, doe bleats, doe-in-heat bleats, moderately toned buck grunts, fawn bleats, buck contact grunts, yearling buck tending grunts and even fawn-in-distress bleats are all proven deer calls. Three easy calls to master—and the ones that bag the most bucks—are the buck contact grunt, doe-in-heat bleat and the series of moderately toned tending buck grunts.

206

Don't be afraid to use your deer call. Sure, improper calling can spook a buck into the next county, but more often than not you will learn something about deer behavior that can be used successfully later in your career. You might, for example, learn how quickly a buck pinpoints your exact location if you and your tree stand are not well camouflaged.

A buck's ears can pinpoint the exact location of a bleat or grunt, so be sure you are well hidden and ready to shoot before you begin calling.

Fawn bleats followed by a few doe bleats can also turn a passing buck around.

207

When blind calling, start your calling sequence with low volume. A buck might be standing nearby and come running in to investigate. If your rendition sounds more like a foghorn, however, a nearby buck might leave the area without you ever knowing he was close at hand.

208

Just because a buck doesn't respond immediately to your calling doesn't mean he is not going to come in. He may take 10 minutes or he might take an hour, so don't give up hope. Indeed, more than one buck has been known to circle around and show up on the downwind side of a tree stand long after the bowhunter relaxed his or her guard.

209

Test the upper limits of every grunt tube you plan to take into the woods with you before you step afield. Some models lose their tonal qualities when you blow hard, causing a squeak that is sure to alert any nearby deer. Sometimes a simple reed adjustment is all it takes to bring the grunt tube back up to specs.

210

Bucks often cruise the edges of major waterways during the rut in their seemingly never-ending search for does in estrous. To narrow your search and pinpoint an exact calling location, look for inlets and bays that funnel bucks close to the shoreline or "around the horn" as they trot from one side of the bay to the other.

211

You'll know the rut has kicked in when you see bucks well after sunrise lingering around feeding areas preferred by family groups of does and fawns. They will be searching for does by scent-checking the edges of openings and by staring off into thick wooded areas. This is a good time to give a roving buck what he is expecting to find—a family group of does and fawns. He will quickly zero in on a couple of fawn bleats followed by a doe bleat or two. Keep your eyes and ears open, but don't be afraid to blind call every 15 minutes or so, either.

In most late-season hunts, doe tags are still valid and, in fact, antlerless deer are often the main quarry.

212

You can set up a tree stand on a downwind edge of the bedding area, or still-hunt in and around the thick stuff. Either way, calling blindly to bucks by using doe-in-heat bleats followed by moderately toned tending buck grunts will work. Stay alert and be ready to shoot at all times because the action can be fast and furious!

213

In most late-season hunts, doe tags are still valid and antlerless deer are often the main quarry. Fawn bleats, for example, can stir a doe's curiosity to the point where she will cautiously come in, whereas a loud blast from a fawn-in-distress specialty call can still bring a doe charging in to rescue a stricken fawn.

214

In most cases, as long as a buck has his rack, he is willing and able to breed. Thus, an estrous doe bleat is always a good choice, with or without an estrous doe decoy positioned facing the buck with her back legs askew. With this set-up it is imperative you choose your tree stand site carefully, making sure you are high above the ground and well concealed.

215

If your call freezes up during the late season, you are calling too much. Slow down, and call more sparingly. A squeaking note now will undoubtedly end your season.

A good-sized rub can be an indication of a big buck.

When Not to Call

216

Do not keep calling if the buck does not respond in a timely manner. He may simply not want to come over for a look-see, so let him go for another day. The last thing you want to do is educate him to your imitation grunts and bleats.

217

Do not call again if the buck appears to have heard your call and is already working his way toward your position. Additional grunts or bleats may only serve to confuse him or, worse, alert him to the fact that you are not another deer.

218

Don't call if the buck is already in bow range or is looking at you or for you just out of range. If he pegs you, the game is over. Instead, hold your ground and let him make the next move. If he turns to walk away, hit him with another note. This is another case where a decoy, buck or doe, can help, as the buck's attention will be riveted on the decoy.

Adding Realism

219

When doubling up on your vocalizations, use a single-purpose call and couple that with notes from a variable grunt tube. It adds a bit of realism to your calling strategy, as it sounds like two distinctly different deer.

Your rendition of a buck "clicking" is effective only during the breeding season. Effective and deadly!

220

If you should snap a twig while still-hunting or walking to your stand and jump a deer, try a confidence call. I like to imitate the soft mew of a fawn, as they always seem to be stumbling about, but avoid the use of a fawn-in-distress call. I can't imagine a scenario where this would help you bag a buck holding steady on "red" alert. A single low doe bleat might also calm down any nearby deer.

221

Learn to double up on your calls. For example, try a doe-in-heat bleat followed by a short series of tending buck grunts. This is a hot combination during the pre-rut as well as the peak of the rut. A lost-fawn bleat followed by a doe-in-heat bleat and then a tending buck grunt can be the ticket when the rut is in full swing. Why? A nearby buck will think a hot doe is about to be bred by a buck in attendance. The "lost" fawn only adds realism to the ruse, as does routinely abandon their fawns while being bred.

Specialty Calls

222

When a buck is in the company of an estrous doe near the very peak of her cycle, he often makes a clicking noise just moments prior to copulation. It sounds much like someone dragging a thumbnail across the teeth of a plastic comb, with each individual click separate and distinct.

When the rut is in full swing, this clicking tells a passing mature buck that a hot doe is somewhere nearby and that mating is about to take place. Use a moderately toned or high-pitched series of clicking, and a sexually experienced trophy buck just might believe that a younger and less mature buck is about to breed—and rush in to take over the breeding rites. A buck decoy with a small to medium rack may help complete the ruse.

223

If you prefer to still-hunt, as I do, and want to call a buck in closer for a clean shot, try a few contact buck grunts followed by your version of a buck making a rub—complete with swaying sapling. It sounds gimmicky, but it works for me at least once a year!

A snort-wheeze is made by a buck exhaling air through his nose in a very specific cadence. Once you have heard it, you won't forget it. It occurs when two bucks of similar status suddenly encounter each other around a food source or a doe near estrous, and serves as a warning to the intruder buck to back off—or there will be a fight. A buck also emits a loud snort-wheeze when a hot doe refuses to stand still long enough to allow breeding to take place.

The snort-wheeze seems to work best during the peak of the rut when mature bucks are tending does. Your rendition of this sound, either alone or along with a tending buck grunt or an estrous doe bleat may be all it takes to pull a mature buck away from a hot doe. But be prepared, as any nearby buck will probably come in looking for a fight!

The buck growl signifies that there is estrous in the air. The sound is beyond a grunt—it is a loud, loud bawling grunt made by a mature buck who is impatiently waiting to breed a doe he has been tending.

When a buck hears another buck growl, he will come to your tree. It works in conjunction with other vocalizations, especially tending buck grunts, the snort-wheeze or even rattling. Used with these other techniques, an imitation buck growl can give the impression that there are several bucks chasing a hot doe, as they so often do during the chase phase.

Call Modifications

Don't let the flexible rubber or plastic ribbed tubing just hang there. One of its functions is to alter the tone. This is accomplished by compressing or stretching the tube as if it were an accordion or by simply cupping your hand over the mouth of the tube, and then blowing. Do this simultaneously, and you can add some interesting tone inflections to your repertoire.

Experiment with tubes of various sizes from different manufacturers to discover several distinct "voices." Inhale/exhale models offer even more options. Indeed, I can get at least four additional tonal ranges with one popular inhale/exhale model by simply attaching the ribbed tubing to a different outlet.

The reed-assembly call offers you the most versatility. You can, for example, securely tape together the two-piece housing and use it separately, or leave it attached to the barrel only. In either instance, exhaling and/or inhaling may produce a softer rendition, which can be important if you're hunting in close quarters, such as from a tree stand overlooking a bedding area or the edge of an uncut cornfield. A loud bellow from a bugle-tipped call would probably alarm nearby bucks in this situation, sending them out of harm's way!

CUSTOMIZE YOUR DEER CALL

"This is it," I thought to myself. "I'm going to get a shot!" I slid my tab around the arrow nock and waited for the buck to step into an opening. Then I watched in horror as the big 8-pointer casually left the trail and trotted past me out of range. I frantically pulled my single-purpose grunt tube from inside my jacket and let out a few quick grunts. For a second I thought I had him, but even a second set of grunts failed to slow his retreat.

In desperation, I twisted the plastic tubing, separating it from the barrel, and looked inside at the reed assembly. I broke the housing holding the plastic reed in place, readjusted the reed and then put the grunt tube back together. It only took a few seconds, but when I looked up, the buck had jumped over a barbed-wire fence some 50 yards (46 m) away.

I had nothing to lose. Much to my astonishment at the time, after one loud grunt from my modified grunt tube the buck stopped dead in his tracks and leaped back over the barbed-wire fence to investigate.

That episode took place in the mid-1980s, and ever since then I have played with grunt tubes to see what makes them grunt, bleat, blat, mew and whine. It should come as no surprise that just as the voices of humans vary in tone, pitch, inflection and duration, so do the "voices" of whitetail. And although modern variable grunt tubes can produce several distinct deer calls, there is always room for improvement in the world of whitetail communication.

229

The ribbed tube also acts like a megaphone, which increases the distance your buck grunts, fawn bleats and doe mews can be heard. However, by flaring the end of the tube, much like an elk bugle, you can increase the volume of the call dramatically. This can be very helpful if you're hunting on the prairie or trying to catch the attention of a buck about to disappear into the next cornfield. Commercial "magnum" variations are now available, or you can modify your present tube by borrowing a length of tubing from your elk bugle.

230

If you're feeling adventurous, you can manipulate the plastic reed to produce several sounds. Generally, if you extend the reed toward your mouth, you'll lower the pitch and vice versa. You can also replace the reed with a homemade version cut from sheets of plastic found at craft supply shops or hardware stores. A small rubber band wrapped around the reed at various distances from the housing produces everything from a fawn bleat to a doe bleat to a buck grunting and clicking, which in effect turns your single-purpose call into a variable.

231

If you don't like the standard barrel lanyard around your neck, attach an alligator clamp to the end of the lanyard, and then clip it to your shirt collar. This allows you to drop the grunt tube from your mouth and out of harm's way when it comes time to shoot.

When calling on windy days or over great distances, try a grunt tube with a flared opening to increase the volume.

Some mini-calls use a rubber band to change the pitch. You can do the same thing with a conventional grunt tube by pulling the reed assembly and wrapping the plastic tongue with a rubber band. The lesson here is simple: Don't discard broken grunt tubes. Save those parts!

For high-tech hunters who want to keep their hands free to shoot, digital deer calls offer many advantages over conventional mouth-blown calls. For example, they can realistically mimic two bucks sparring.

Digital Calls

232

With a digital deer call, you don't have to worry about a poor imitation when the right situation presents itself. Electronic deer calls are accurate renditions of whitetail vocalizations.

233

Digital deer-calling devices offer several advantages over mouth-blown devices: They don't freeze up, and because of their larger size you're not likely to lose them on the way to your hunting grounds, either. Plus, you can use them in conjunction with drag rags, scent bombs and decoys.

234

Digital deer calls offer consistent quality. You don't have to worry about squeaking or hitting a sour note if you become overwhelmed with excitement. Every rendition is a perfect imitation of the vocalization you want to reproduce—each and every time.

235

You can also tinker with the barrel and the reed assembly. The reed assembly is attached to the ribbed tubing and then inserted into the barrel. I prefer wood barrels over plastic versions because the buck grunts and the doe bleats resonate more realistically. Besides sounding better, hardwood barrels are not nearly as noisy if you accidentally hit one with your bow or gun.

236

Use a digital deer call to "throw" those grunts and bleats, thus directing the buck's attention away from your position. Experienced deer hunters know that any sound, no matter how slight, will rivet a suspicious buck's attention to the source of the call.

237

There is a wider range of other deer sounds available that can be used during the open season. In addition to two bucks sparring, for example, and the standard grunts and bleats, some models offer the pawing sounds of a buck making a scrape and the rubbing sounds of a buck making a rub! These natural deer sounds also attract bucks, sounds that you cannot get from a standard grunt tube.

238

Use a digital call when a buck hangs up just out of range. Remaining motionless lowers your odds of being picked off by a buck's incredible eyesight and increases your chance of getting a suspicious buck to take a step or two in your direction.

Conventional deer calls sound unrealistic inside enclosed blinds and are more likely to spook deer rather than bring them in close. This is where a digital system with a speaker positioned outside the blind is your best bet.

The best deer hunters I know practice calling turkeys, ducks and predators during the off-season. If you can call fox into close range, as these teenagers did, then calling bucks to within bow range should be a snap!

239

You can make all sounds more realistic by setting the digital deer caller on the ground behind a tree trunk near your stand, or in a ravine some distance from your stand. The sounds of a buck pawing a scrape, rubbing a tree or sparring with another buck is certainly more credible when the scraping and pawing and grinding sounds are at ground zero and not 15 feet (4.5 m) up in the air.

240

You can more easily give a nearby passing buck the one-two punch with a digital deer call. During the peak rut, for example, a mature buck on the loose might be enticed to change course if he hears something he's looking for. In this case, the sounds of a doe near estrous followed immediately by the "urp-urp-urp" of

a young buck in attendance might lure that old buck into shooting range. And you can do it all by remote control!

241

You do not have to hang your bow or rifle up to make the call(s). Instead you can sit confidently with a nocked arrow or stand at port arms with a loaded firearm and let the digital deer emit the vocalizations of your choice. Why is this so important? It often takes only one note to lure a nearby buck into range and that buck can come in on a full charge, giving you no time to drop your call and grab your weapon. Indeed, more "hot" bucks have escaped unscathed simply because the caller was not ready to shoot when the buck arrived unexpectedly on the scene.

Rattling

242

On opening day try a bit of rattling. Not hard and harsh, mind you, but soft and easy to imitate two bucks sparring in order to test each other's strengths and weaknesses. A rattle bag seems to work best here. Just rub the bag back and forth between your hands for 10 or 15 seconds at a time, and then grab your bow. This low-level grinding is apt to tweak the curiosity of any buck passing nearby.

243

During the early season, bucks can be very territorial. About 5 to 10 seconds of very light rattling with a rattle bag can bring an unseen buck to your stand in a jiffy. If he is already in view, a single "urp" from your grunt tube may also do the trick.

A good place to look for fresh scrapes and rub lines is along old logging roads.

244

The pre-rut is one of the best times to rattle-in a buck. If scrapes and ruts are just appearing, use your rattling horns in a tickling and slow-grinding fashion. This is more likely to lure a lone rutting buck into shooting range. Save your loud, foot-stomping aggressive antler rattling for the late pre-rut and the peak of the rut when buck fights are more common.

245

If you are hunting from the ground and a buck hangs up just out of range, try grunting, bleating, mewing or rattling from a different location. This is a great maneuver if you can pull it off without being seen. Raking an antler up and down a tree trunk, or pawing at the ground with a stick might be all it takes then to get that buck to finally commit himself to the set-up.

Knock-down-and-drag-out buck fights do not occur in the early season. Bucks will, however, spar with each other. This is when a rattle bag and light rattling are most effective.

DOES SIZE MATTER?

While some hunters believe you need a set of trophy antlers to rattle a mature buck into shooting range, it has not been my experience. In fact, any two bucks sparring seems to attract the attention of does, spikes and button bucks as well as the local dominant buck. Indeed, I once used a 6-point rack to rattle in a 150-class Montana buck.

I do suggest, however, you use fairly fresh rattling antlers, as opposed to a sun-bleached and porous set of "bones," and that you remove the brow tines so you don't crush your fingers while rattling.

And yes, synthetic antlers work, too.

HOW TO BECOME A DEAD SHOT WITH BOW & ARROW

Being a dead shot with a bow and arrow under hunting conditions is not the same as stacking arrows in the bull's-eye at 20 yards (18 m) on the target range—not by a long shot. Why? There are variables in the hunting woods that you don't regularly encounter at the practice range.

Indeed, being a crack shot at the clubhouse in no way guarantees you a pass-through on the buck of your dreams. There are many skills you need to hone razor sharp before you can become a dead shot with a bow and arrow.

246

There is no doubt that hours and hours of practice at the range helps you learn how to properly grip the bow, then come to full draw without dropping the arrow off the rest, hold steady on target, use your back muscles and, finally, execute a perfect release complete with follow-through. Practice promotes muscle growth and muscle memory, and if you practice religiously you will eventually be packing tight groups from 20 to 40 yards (18 to 37 m) and beyond.

Unfortunately, the problem with this kind of practice is that you rarely get to stand tall facing a relaxed big game animal in the wild. And you rarely get to take your sweet time releasing a razor-tipped shaft at its vitals. In many cases you barely have time to estimate the distance and come to full draw before the animal turns and walks away.

So, how should you practice? After you master the basics at the clubhouse, re-create a realistic bowhunting scenario and start shooting your bow from unorthodox positions.

Practice on a target range can teach you the basics, but it doesn't adequately prepare you for a shot under actual hunting conditions.

247

For still-hunting, begin your practice sessions by shooting from awkward positions, such as kneeling behind a log, stooping under a branch or sitting on a steep sidehill.

248

Learn the importance of using a bubble level when taking practice shots over uneven terrain. Keep in mind that your level must be perpendicular to the bowstring. You may need to shim it if it's not.

249

If you don't have a level, cant the bow into the hill when shooting on a slope. The steeper the slope, the more acute the angle.

250

If you don't have a bubble level and time is of the essence, try using a nearby tree trunk as a guide to canting the bow correctly.

251

Practice shooting sitting down facing the target as well as quartering away from the target. In addition, practice twisting your torso around the tree trunk and taking a shot right next to the tree. Imagine a buck passing by from every conceivable angle, and then diligently practice that shot.

Imagine a buck passing by from every conceivable angle, and then practice, practice, practice.

Dense foliage or twigs and branches can make a deer seem farther away.

252

Be sure to practice under low-light conditions so you learn the importance of having a peep sight with a wide aperture.

253

During your practice sessions you may notice that you do not always come to full draw. And even if you do come to full draw, your bowstring might be regularly striking your arm or wrist. Complete misses or episodic poor arrow flight may be due to not coming to full draw, in part because your draw length is a bit too long. Many accuracy problems can be solved by simply shortening your draw length an inch or two (2.5 or 5 cm).

Yardage Estimation

254

A crucial skill you need to develop is learning to accurately estimate the distance of the shot. Stump shooting and 3-D tournaments can help sharpen your estimation skills, but don't make the mistake many bowhunters do at these events. If you're going to shoot from an unorthodox position, like kneeling or sitting down, then guess the shooting distance from that position—not standing up. Things look mighty different when you are at or below eye level to a whitetail.

255

A buck appears farther away than he really is when you are positioned in bright sunlight and shooting into a "tunnel" of dark shadows, or if you're standing in the shadows and shooting at an exceptionally large animal in an open field.

256

Here is an exercise that can help you judge distances more accurately. First, learn how many of your natural steps it takes to equal 10 yards (9 m). In my case it's 14 steps equals 10 yards (9 m), and 28 steps add up to 20 yards (18 m). Now when I want to know the distance to a certain object, I count out to that object in my mind in 10-yard intervals using a rock, leaf or branch as a 10-yard marker.

257

Make a game out of judging distances in your backyard with some friends using a quality range finder. Simply "eyeball" the distance to an object in the yard, such as the mailbox or an ornamental tree, and then check your estimate against the readout on the range finder. You should see improvement during your first practice session.

Noted Vermont whitetail expert Jeff Grab says, "Keep in mind that you rarely have an opportunity to put a range finder on a big game animal before the shot. Rutting whitetails have a habit of showing up from out of the blue when you least expect them."

258

You must be very cautious when shooting up- or downhill at acute angles. The measured distance either downhill or uphill may be 25 yards (23 m) on your range finder, for example, but the actual shooting distance is far less.

259

The rule of thumb is to gauge the distance as if the animal were on the same plane as you. If the deer is standing downhill next to a tree, don't estimate the distance to the tree's trunk, but rather to a point on the tree that is perpendicular to your position. If you're thinking about taking an uphill shot, "look into the hill" and imagine where that animal would be standing if there were no hill present. In both cases, deer standing uphill and downhill from you are really closer than they appear.

No matter your weapon of choice, the more acute the angle, the shorter the actual shooting distance.

NEVER GIVE UP

I watched the two bucks exit the green field at pink light and slip into a block of planted pines. I circled downwind and glassed a hedgerow that connected that block of pines to a 100-acre (40 ha) stand of hardwoods 200 yards (183 m) to the west. Just as I was about to look elsewhere, the two bucks exited the planted pines and began feeding along the edge of the hedgerow.

When they disappeared into the hardwoods, I hoofed it across the field and cautiously entered the stand of acorn-bearing oak trees. The bucks were gone, but there were acorns, droppings and tracks everywhere. I turned and slowly worked my way into the wind, hoping to bump into another buck. An hour later I was about to call it quits for the day when something caught my eye some 40 yards (37 m) away. It was the throat patch of a wide-racked buck feeding crosswind to me. I crept forward and dropped to one knee, and when the buck's head dropped to the ground I pulled a carbon hunting shaft from my quiver, nocked it and brought my bow to full draw.

I found him piled up a short distance away.

All it takes is one pencil-thin twig to send your arrow off into the wild blue yonder.

260

Leave your bow at the clubhouse and walk a 3-D course with a friend, each of you writing down your estimated distance and the actual distance to each foam animal. When you complete the course, add up the differences to see who did the better job. A little competition can sharpen your distance-estimation skills.

261

I have a friend who teaches his brain to recognize a certain distance by repetition. Allen Miraglia, owner of Scrubby Buck Archery, does this by staring at a telephone pole that is exactly 27 yards (25 m) away while he is on the computer. "That distance is burned into my 'hard drive,' and is easy to recognize in the wild," he explains.

262

In the hunting world weeds, leaves and brush can sometimes interfere with broadhead flight and accuracy. It is common knowledge that a twig can easily send a vaned or feathered shaft astray, but do you know what effect goldenrod has on arrow flight? What about a cluster of oak leaves? With realistic practice you soon realize that the closer the weeds or leaves are to the deer, the less effect they have on accuracy or broadhead flight.

263

Not sure if an overhanging branch will block your shot? The trick here is to "arc" your arrow's shaft past that troublesome branch, and the way you do that is by "pinning" the offending branch. For example, let's say that you have a 35-yard (32 m) shot, but an overhanging branch 20 yards (18 m) in front of you seems to be blocking the shot. Put your 20-yard pin on the branch, and then look to see if your 35-yard pin offers you ample clearance. If it does, let her rip!

264

You can't expect to down a deer if you don't shoot, but being a dead shot means being a responsible shot. There is no honor in wounding and then losing a big game animal because you elected to take a "Hail Mary" shot rather than wait for a closer shot or a better angle.

If you shoot and just wound him, you will probably never see that buck again. On the other hand, if you pass up a low percentage opportunity, your chances of seeing that buck again on another day are good.

265

Knowing when to shoot and when to pass is a learned skill, based on experience and time spent afield. This is where your target buddies lose out. The best target shots I know spend most of their free time on the range fine-tuning their equipment so they can shoot bull's-eyes at 50, 60 and even 70 yards (46, 55, 64 m).

On the other hand, the best bowhunters I know spend most of their free time in the woods looking for deer and deer sign. Their goal is to locate ambush zones where they can take high-percentage shots at animals well within their effective accuracy range.

HOW TO BECOME A DEAD SHOT WITH FIREARMS

Although shooting 1-inch (2.5 cm) bull's-eyes at 100 yards (91 m) at the target range is a good beginning, it does not automatically make you a crack hunting shot in the deer woods.

A buck can appear suddenly, giving you precious little time to aim and squeeze the trigger. The lighting can also be poor and, to make matters more difficult, the kill zone may be partially obscured by brush. When you add buck fever, it is no wonder so many deer escape unscathed.

There are as many good deer rifles as there are good deer hunters. The secret is to match the gun to your style of hunting.

266

No one gun does it all, and if you're a serious deer hunter, you may need to own more than one specialty gun to cover all your hunting needs. There is a place in the deer woods for bolt actions, lever actions, pump actions, single shot actions and semi-auto actions. Each can be fitted with a variety of open sight configurations as well as fixed and variable telescopic sights. The trick is to match the gun to the terrain, style of hunting and weather conditions expected on the day of the hunt.

267

Horror stories abound about deer hunters trying to be a crack shot with an unfamiliar weapon. One way to gain familiarity is to go to the rifle range and shoot, shoot and then shoot some more. In the process you will learn about proper sight picture, controlled breathing, trigger pull, muzzle blast, recoil, quick reloading and other necessary shooting skills.

268

One of the hallmarks of being a dead shot in the deer woods is to know how important it is to find a steady rest before you squeeze the trigger on a racked deer.

Don't relax around a downed deer. Check to make sure it is dead first before you smile for the camera. It might just be stunned!

269

You can improve your basic shooting skills even more by target practicing the same way you hunt. Start at the range by bringing your gun to your shoulder as quickly as possible, as if you just jumped a buck, and then shooting at a deer-size target. You will soon acquire a better feel for the gun, including where you should rest your head in relation to the preferred sight system and the importance of having a sight picture in your head before you raise your gun. This is not to say you want to snap shoot in the deer woods, but the quicker you can get the gun on target, the more time you have to take precise and steady aim at a wild animal.

270

Set up a target range much like an archer's 3-D course. A gully or ravine will give you a wide assortment of places to safely shoot from. Taking shots at unknown distances and from unorthodox angles will undoubtedly help you hone your shooting skills.

When to Shoot, When Not to Shoot

271

Being a good shot means more than knowing when to shoot; it also means avoiding low percentage opportunities. If you can't nail a rabbit or a flushing grouse at 25 yards (23 m) with a scattergun, for example, what makes you think you can take a galloping buck through the lungs at 100 yards (91 m)?

272

The best hunters never take their eye off a downed buck. They walk directly over to him ready to shoot again in case he gets up. In fact, don't ever hesitate to take a second or even a third follow-up shot.

I always walk up on a downed deer with my rifle or shotgun at port arms, and if I think the deer might still be alive, I shoot him again. The cost of a deer slug or big game cartridge is cheap insurance compared to losing a buck!

273

When you catch a buck trotting across a wooded ridge, don't start blasting, but rather look ahead for an opening and calmly take your shot when he steps into the clear. A crack shot takes only high-percentage shots and hits what he or she is aiming at every time.

Kneel down, take advantage of your sling and use a rest whenever possible.

274

Test your gun's safety. Have a competent gunsmith take a look at it if you can't disengage it quietly.

275

After your deer rifle is sighted in and shooting solid groups, step away from the bench and shoot a series of three-shot groups from a standing, sitting, kneeling and prone position at 100, 150 and 200 yards (91, 182, 273 m). You will realize that when you shoot from the other positions, your groups are much better than from the standing position.

There is a lesson here, and it is a basic one. Never shoot standing up when you can sit or kneel, and never shoot sitting or kneeling when you can shoot from the prone position. Gun wobble is the culprit here, and you can reduce it by simply increasing the number of pressure points in your stance.

276

No mater what you do, gun wobble will not disappear completely. You need more than just a solid stance, and for some hunters it comes in

the form of a sling. It's amazing how much more accurate you can shoot when you wrap your arms around a gun strap. It takes practice, and you may need to readjust your sling as you don bulkier clothing for the winter months, but its ability to help stabilize a wandering gun barrel under a wide variety of shooting positions will be worth all your efforts. Indeed, a sling can come in handy when still-hunting, sitting over crop fields or even when hunkered down on a hardwoods slope waiting for a rutting buck to pass by.

277

Jim Massett, former president of the New York State Big Buck Club, is a deep woods deer hunter and expert tracker. When he's on the trail of a trophy buck, he unslings his rifle and stuffs it in his pocket to avoid the temptation of slinging his deer rifle over his shoulder. "It only takes a second for a buck to appear and then disappear, and if you are carrying your deer rifle over your shoulder rather than in your hand(s), that buck can be gone and out of your life forever before you get your rifle off your shoulder," Massett explains.

I heed Massett's advice and do not sling my rifle over my shoulder when actively pursuing whitetails, but I do keep the sling attached to my rifle in case I need to use it to help steady a long shot.

278

Remember how accurate you were when you shot from the prone position rather than sitting, kneeling or standing? You can be even more accurate if you bolt on a bipod or employ a set of shooting sticks. This solid three-point stance is nearly unbeatable for long-range accuracy, and is thus especially useful when hunting along power lines, gas lines and other rights-of-way as well as over bean fields, rolling prairie lands and big woods clear-cuts.

279

It always amazes me to see hunters on the target ranges just prior to the buck opener. For most, this is the only time of the year they shoot their deer guns which is hardly enough time to hone their basic shooting skills.

Fortunately, there is an alternative strategy: practicing at home an hour or so a week with an air rifle. These practice sessions can help you become a more accurate shot without suffering the recoil or cost of shooting a big game rifle, shotgun or muzzleloader.

280

When hunting thick swamps and farmland brush lots, a 1.5x-5x variable or a fixed 2.5x scope is more than sufficient. A larger power scope will give you a narrower field of view, making it quite difficult to pick up a nearby standing buck. In fact, I've shot plenty of racked deer from 100 to 175 yards (91 to 160 m) with my variable set at 1.5x, leading me to believe a higher power scope is unnecessary under most circumstances.

SCOPE CARE

One season I slipped on a wet slope and fell on top of my scoped '06—hard. I was sure I had knocked the scope out of whack, but by the time I got back to camp it was raining hard and too dark to visit the camp's target range.

I didn't sleep much that night. I had to test fire the gun, for my own peace of mind, before I could confidently step back into the woods. Fortunately, the following morning I discovered that although the scope took a beating it was still dead-on at 100 yards (91 m).

Today things are different—thank goodness! Products like the Laser Bore Alignment Kit from Laserlyte allow you to check if your scope is still on its mark without shooting your gun. It can even be accomplished inside after supper while your buddies are doing the dishes!

It's all done with a battery-operated laser light that is first inserted into an alignment tool and then slid into the muzzle of your deer gun. This effectively aligns the laser light with the center of the bore axis. A laser dot is then projected onto a small reflective target telling you instantly if the sights have been moved. (You simply compare the position of that dot with measurements you took earlier when the gun was first sighted in.)

If need be, you can use the laser dot to re-sight the gun close enough (4 inches/10 cm at 100 yards/91 m) to hunt in the morning, with final adjustments made later at the range. This is definitely a tool that every deer camp should have on hand for emergencies.

The best shots are familiar with their equipment and hunt year-round. And the very best shots start shooting at an early age.

281

Don't overlook the advantages a peep sight offers, especially in thick tangles on moving deer. Winchester, Marlin, Henry and Savage offer lever-action carbines that can be fitted with aftermarket peep sights that are just deadly in these situations.

282

You can effectively still-hunt and snow-track racked bucks when the weather is downright nasty. Rain keeps the leaves quiet underfoot for the stop-and-go hunter and swirling snow allows a tracker to walk right up on an unsuspecting buck.

A fogged or rain-drenched scope is almost useless under these conditions. A rifle fitted with See-Thru or Tip-Off mounts, however, can be a season saver because they allow you to switch to a wide-aperture sighting system that is not so adversely affected by inclement weather.

283

Once the deer season begins, be sure to keep your firearm and scope safe from bangs and bruises.

284

Even if your deer rifle is a tack driver, and you are shooting it like a pro, that doesn't mean you are going to automatically connect on the buck of your dreams. You must also be mentally prepared to make the shot without hesitation when the opportunity presents itself.

Maintain your sight picture for a full second before squeezing off a round.

285

Be ready to take the shot when a buck steps into view. I can't tell you how many bucks I let walk when in retrospect I should have shot, all because I was looking for a bigger rack. Know what your minimums are before you step afield, and then take the shot when the opportunity presents itself.

286

Aiming at a deer's entire body will almost certainly result in a miss, or worse, a bad hit. When you decide the deer in front of you is a "shooter," visualize the crosshairs or sight bead on a small part of the body before you raise your gun, a tuft of hair behind the "elbow," for example, and then maintain that sight picture for a full second before squeezing off a round. It is a deadly technique.

SECRET BUCK TRAILS

So how do you locate secret buck trails and hidden corridors? They have several common characteristics you can prepare yourself to look for on your next scouting trip.

287

The first function of a buck trail is to protect bucks as they travel around their home range. In this regard, bucks take advantage of various terrain features, available ground cover and prevailing winds to move undetected between bedding areas and feeding grounds.

Sometimes a wooded ridgeline, a brush-choked ravine or a gentle slope guides them to their destination, while at other times a low spot in a meadow overgrown with goldenrod, briars and Queen Anne's lace does the trick. Think concealment, think safety, think survival, and you'll soon discover secret buck trails.

288

The second function of a buck trail is to help save calories. Bucks simply cannot afford to burn energy inefficiently. Thus, buck trails are often the easiest, quickest, shortest and least stressful routes available. For example, if you were to cross a creek, where is the shallowest water? Where are the banks less steep? Is there a gentle slope leading in and out of the water? Learn to look for these clues and others like them, and you'll discover even more corridors.

289

Be aware that buck trails are generally seasonal in nature. As new food sources mature—such as acorns, beechnuts and various agricultural crops—current buck trails are re-routed in order to take advantage of these emerging sources of nutrition. This means that a buck trail that's hot during the week may be temporarily abandoned by week's end.

290

Keep in mind that the first two functions of buck trails are not mutually exclusive. That is, the route bucks take to a feeding location or bedding site is often the one that is both most direct and offers the most concealment.

291

Most hunters come across several types of whitetail habitat. The secrets of open-country corridors can be the most difficult to unravel, but a few days scouting before you bowhunt will be time well spent. Breeding trails are seasonal, but when the rut is in full swing you can often catch a buck flat-footed here anytime during legal shooting hours.

Can't find any buck sign? Head toward the water!

Learn to identify secret buck trails, and you will shoot more bucks.

292

When leaf drop occurs, the amount of cover afforded by brush and saplings changes, too, forcing deer to use alternate pathways to seasonal food supplies and bedding cover. This is one explanation of why deer seem to suddenly disappear early in the season. The bucks haven't left the area, and you probably didn't spook them either. Their change in travel simply reflects the changes in cover and food sources that nature is now providing.

293

Secret buck trails are often located near water. If deer are in the area, you will find evidence along the edges of swamps and beaver dams as well as the shorelines of rivers, lakes and ponds. Why? Not only is food available here in the form of fresh shoots in the spring and browse in late fall, but generally there is also plenty of cover year-round.

TRAIL FUNNELS

I was about ready to give up. I had been scouting a several-thousand-acre (hectare) forested tract that I knew held plenty of whitetails, but deer sign was scarce even after two mornings of serious scouting. I was beginning to wonder if all the bucks hadn't been shot during the previous fall fusillade, when I stumbled upon a large set of deer prints—and then another and another.

I followed the trail uphill in the wet leaves for quite a distance before I realized that the tracks were leading to a suspected bedding area. Suddenly, there were snorts and flags everywhere as a half-dozen or so deer ran back down the ridge to the creek bottom below.

I looked around for a while and then backtracked another set of deer prints to an old apple orchard. There was plenty of sign there, too, enough for me to get a little excited about opening day, even though it was still several weeks away.

Since that scouting trip 25 or more years ago, I've learned to zero in on those features that seem to funnel bucks from one end of their home range to another. Indeed, even though they may live on a 1,000-acre (405 ha) farm or 2,000-acre (809 ha) block of wilderness, they don't move freely. For a variety of reasons, much of the area may go "unused" for months or even years at a time. Instead, deer seem to utilize secret trails and hidden corridors to help them get around unnoticed.

You see, bucks travel from bedding areas to feeding grounds by wandering through a narrow section of their home range. They're less likely to be picked off by a predator here because their route is less predictable. It is certainly safer than plodding along a single trail like family groups of does and fawns are apt to do. And since they are usually the only deer to take this general route, there are often fewer tracks and rolled-over leaves to let you know they've passed by.

294

Secret buck trails are also circular in nature. While family groups of does and fawns may very well travel back and forth using the same trail or system of trails, bucks quite often do not. Rather, bucks use one trail in the evening to reach a preferred food source and another trail the next morning to return to a preferred bedding area. Still other trails are used strictly on a nocturnal basis.

Terrain

295

Ravines that run up and down the mountain and saddles between two peaks are two good places to look for buck trails, as are spurs and gentle slopes that connect high peaks to creek bottoms, clear-cuts and farm fields at the base of the mountain.

296

The best way to locate secret trails is by scouting the area on foot, but to get a leg up on where to start, invest in some topo maps and aerial photographic images. Once you pencil in probable food sources and suspected bedding areas, preferred buck trails should quickly become evident.

297

In general you'll find that ground cover dominates the flow and direction of buck trails. Indeed, abandoned farm fields now overrun with goldenrod, briars, dogwood, hardwood saplings and small evergreens are always candidates for a thorough scouring.

298

Keep in mind that farmland food sources often have their own trails. Bucks, for example, rarely walk out into the middle of an open field and begin to feed. Rather, they enter an alfalfa lot or bean field near a section of heavy cover and start feeding along the edge of the field. Only when darkness prevails do they venture into the open flats.

In the early season when food is the key to locating racked deer, an ambush site along a heavily wooded section adjacent to an open feeding area or inside a hedgerow that juts across an open feeding area are two excellent sites for a tree stand. Unfortunately, you'll likely have only one opportunity in these locations. If you spook a buck from one of these open ambush sites, your chances of getting a second opportunity are slim.

299

The trick to locating breeding trails is to first know the exact whereabouts of several bedding areas preferred by family groups of does and fawns, and the feeding areas they're using as the rut peaks.

A rutting buck goes from one known concentration of does to the next in search of a doe near estrous. Once he has scoured a bedding area without success, he will then bee-line it to the nearest feeding site or bedding area. If he is unsuccessful here, then he goes straight to the next bedding/feeding site and so on until he rounds up a hot doe. These breeding trails are direct, often crossing wide open spaces, and thus are designed primarily to save calories.

Breeding trails are direct, often crossing wide open spaces and thus are designed primarily to save calories.

300

Do you want to locate some breeding trails before the rut occurs again? Pencil in known doe bedding and feeding locations on a topo map or an aerial photograph. Then draw lines connecting them. Later, during a scouting mission, look for a combination of old and newer rubs along these lines to verify your suspicions.

301

Get on a knoll near a food source, and glass at first light and again as the sun goes down. This is when the prairie suddenly comes alive with deer. Your job is to watch bucks as they use every nuance in elevation and every bit of scrub brush as cover to safely work their way back and forth between feeding and bedding sites. Cover is more important here than saving calories.

Chapter 3

THE PEAK OF THE RUT

It was a most memorable morning afield. I had seen nine antlered deer including a wide-racked 10-pointer that dashed onto posted property, and a dandy 8-pointer I later missed with my bow. There were bucks seemingly everywhere, and they were moving, too, as it was the peak of the breeding season.

What helped make this morning so special, however, was the fact that I had finally figured out how to take advantage of all this daytime commotion. I learned that whether you hunt with archery tackle, black powder or modern firearm, you have to drop some old habits and develop a few new tactics if you expect to consistently score during the peak of the rut.

You must be prepared to shoot a deer at all times of the day.

301

Several seasons back I spent the morning hours still-hunting with archery tackle along a steep ravine. By noon I was tired and hungry and decided to walk directly back to my 4x4. I had in essence given up for the day.

I then made the mistake of entering an open hay lot without first checking it for deer. When I looked up, I saw not one or two but three bucks staring at me less than 40 yards (37 m) away. They had been walking along the edge of that open field looking for does in the middle of the day and saw me before I saw them. They escaped before I could nock an arrow, proving that you must be mentally prepared for a close encounter at all times during the peak of the rut.

302

As the days grow shorter, bucks spend more and more daylight hours searching for an estrous doe. Soon most of the available does will be coming into heat, and the bucks will be running crazily here and there in an effort to make a connection.

What does this mean? If you want to see bucks, forgo the techniques you relied upon during the early season and the pre-rut. For example, one of the hottest tactics for tree stand hunters during the pre-rut is to sit overlooking a primary scrape. But if the bucks are checking out doe feeding areas, doe bedding areas and the trails connecting the two for estrous does, and there are plenty of does coming in heat, then why should they return to a primary scrape? Well, aside from a few exceptions, they rarely do!

303

Bucks are now with a doe for long periods, bedding where she beds and eating where she eats for up to three or more days in a row. Thus, there is little use setting up an ambush outside one of the buck's preferred pre-rut or early-season bedding zones. Nor would it be a good idea to set up on a trail dotted with big rubs, the ones that connect his preferred feeding areas to his bedroom. And don't bother trying to ambush him near one of his near-dawn or pre-sunset staging areas, either. Why? He is simply not bedding or feeding in these places anymore—he's out chasing does!

Cornfields become deer sanctuaries unless you're on top of it.

304

When the rut is on, the best time to be afield is any time you can get away! The hunting can be exciting at first light, noontime and just before dark—and all hours in between! If you oversleep or the alarm jolts you out of bed an hour late, don't roll over and go back to sleep thinking the day is ruined. During the rut, you just never know when a monster buck will come sauntering into view.

305

Remember that to locate a willing partner, rutting bucks often expand their territories from 1 or 2 square miles (2.6 to 5.2 sq km) to 10 or 12 square miles (26 to 31 sq km), especially when deer densities are low.

306

Researchers like Charles Alsheimer have proved that rutting behavior is heavily influenced by the moon: "Deer activity begins increasing when the second full moon after the autumnal equinox [rutting moon] arrives and peaks a couple days after the third quarter. Breeding data has shown that the majority of breeding activity occurs from the third to first quarter that follows the rutting moon."

307

Bucks often use the same breeding routes year after year. Look for a rub line connecting doe hot spots with trees that have been rubbed for several years to confirm your suspicions.

308

Bucks often walk parallel to a fence line, ridge or creek bed as they look for estrous does. They also rub along that line, again often scarring the same tree or clump of trees for several years in a row. Try to locate a "hub" where several buck trails cross, such as near a steep ravine or edge of a swamp; now you have a good stand site for the peak of the rut.

LOCATING NOCTURNAL BUCKS

What makes a buck go nocturnal? In many cases it is human intrusion. Bowhunters, for example, may spook him during their pre-season scouting forays by leaving their scent on his runways or near his feeding areas. They might even jump him from his bed, causing the buck to bed elsewhere for at least a while. Of course, hikers, bird watchers and small game hunters can also push bucks into the twilight zone, as can those who spotlight open areas at night.

Large unharvested corn lots are good hiding places for you to set up.

309

If you're not seeing a particular buck anymore, that doesn't necessarily mean he has gone nocturnal, assuming of course he is still alive. A buck may have been visible all summer long, but as soon as he sheds his velvet, he prefers solitude and remains bedded down for as long as possible during daylight hours.

310

Of course, that buck doesn't have to feed in the same meadow or farm field every night, which makes your job even tougher.

311

A buck can also change his bedding area, and as a result you aren't as likely to see him. As corn plants grow, for example, bucks move off the ridges and out of the swamps to take advantage of the cover offered by mature plants. Large unharvested corn lots are such good hiding places you may not see the bucks that live here until the corn is picked.

312

In some cases an absent buck is simply feeding elsewhere. A wind storm may knock the season's first mast crop to the forest floor. Once the deer find them, they will abandon other food sources, and return again and again to feed on the acorns, beechnuts, hickory nuts, apples, etc, until they are all gone. You must change your routine to take advantage of these new conditions.

313

A word of caution: If you fail to get a shot at a buck that has gone nocturnal, and either jump him or spook him with your scent, you may as well look for another deer to hunt, as this buck is definitely unkillable now during legal shooting hours.

314

Another reason you may have trouble locating a certain buck is that he's now bedding closer to a primary food source, sometimes within just a few yards (meters) of where he eats. Since they now spend less time traveling between bedding and feeding grounds, they are less likely to be seen during daylight hours.

315

Bucks may bed some distance away and simply not arrive to feed until later in the evening. Stay in your stand until hunting hours are closed!

316

Some bucks go nocturnal as a function of age. Indeed, most bucks past three years of age are shy. Yet even yearling bucks can go nocturnal after their first encounter with a human, which is another reason to avoid contact with bucks during your pre-season scouting sessions.

317

The first step to locating a buck that has pulled the disappearing act is to get a better feel for his home territory. Try glassing for him in open feeding areas after sunset and before sunrise around open feeding areas.

318

A buck may have found a secondary food source, and will feed there for an hour before continuing on to his primary food source.

To relocate a nocturnal buck, glass suspected feeding areas, travel routes and bedding areas before dawn and after dusk.

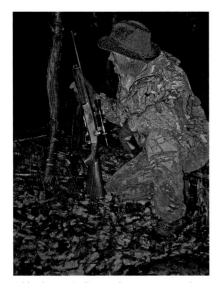

Old rubs can indicate where a nocturnal buck is now hanging out.

To get a crack at a nocturnal buck, locate his daytime bedding area without disturbing him—and set up as close as you dare.

319

If that buck is indeed nocturnal, he is not arriving on the scene until it is dead dark—an hour or more after sundown. You'll need good (read: expensive) binoculars to see him now. In most states you cannot be afield with a weapon at this time. That should give you a clue as to how dark it is when nocturnal bucks begin moving about.

320

If you have an idea where the Old Boy is bedding, look for a scrape line (or a rub line) that he uses to exit or enter his secret bedding zone, and then be there the very next time you expect him to be there. A combination of estrous doe bleats and tending buck grunts might cause him to delay his bedding plans or even rise from his bed early, and then move closer to the source of the calls for a better look.

321

Your best opportunity to ambush a nocturnal buck will be the very first time you set up on him. If he is a mature buck, light rattling or buck contact grunts might be all it takes to tweak his territorial instincts. Indeed, he might just leave a bit early to see what all the commotion is about, and give you a legal shot.

322

Be ready to give up several evenings of prime hunting time to locate or relocate a nocturnal buck.

323

A mature buck usually rubs bigger trees, from 2 to 7 or more inches (5 or 18 cm) in diameter, but when they're removing their velvet, they often use a small bush. These signposts are harder to locate but often give you good clues about where the buck is feeding and bedding.

324

If all else fails, rely on old rubs and past sightings to help you pinpoint a buck's present whereabouts. If he is still alive, he's probably using the same trails and feeding in the same general area as during the previous season.

325

To locate the ideal ambush point for a nocturnal buck, deduce the whereabouts of his daytime lair using tracks, scrapes, rubs, trails, previous sightings, the lay of the land, amount of undergrowth and past experience.

326

The real secret to getting a shot at any nocturnal buck is to set up as close as you dare to his bedding area, not his feeding grounds.

THE DOE FACTOR

The peak of the rut is supposed to be one of the best times to ambush a racked deer. Yet season after season buck hunters get skunked during the breeding season because they can not find a buck.

Indeed, bucks are no longer feeding anywhere on a regular basis, and they have certainly stopped bedding in the thick stuff in favor of open fields and thin strips of brush. And in most cases they have even abandoned their hot scrapes and scrape lines, too.

What is going on? Testosterone levels are high and bucks have only one thing now on their minds: procreation.

If you want to get a crack at a racked buck during the peak of the rut, then hunt the does. After all, that's what the bucks are doing!

327

During the summer months glass open meadows and pastures, as well as bean lots and alfalfa fields, to learn where the does enter and exit these feeding areas. Later take the time to backtrack several doe runs to find probable bedding grounds. Your goal is to be as familiar with the local doe population as you are with the local buck population.

328

One of the best ways to locate a rutting buck is to glass an open feeding area such as a cut corn lot or hay mowing at first light. You'll find bucks standing on high points and looking for feeding does, as well as sniffing their way along the edges of the field hoping to come across a hot scent trail. Look, too, for flashes of white in the pre-dawn darkness. Depending on her breeding status, a doe often runs from an amorous buck, giving you glimpses of her bouncing flag and underbelly as she high-tails it for cover.

Be on-site by first light, and glass edges of cornfields and open feeding areas preferred by family groups of does and fawns.

Buck, doe and fawn decoys can be used to entice a rutting buck into range.

329

Another strategy gaining popularity in some deer hunting circles is the use of a bedded doe decoy to help lure a rutting buck in close for a shot, doused with doe-in-heat urine and placed in plain sight along a well-used doe exit trail or travel route.

330

Once you secure the field, still-hunt just outside the field and along the perimeter. You never quite know when a rutting buck will materialize, so I will often circle a field again and again, if the prevailing winds allow, until the last feeding doe exits the field.

331

If you find that there are several exit routes, which is common when you're hunting large feeding areas, then a little scouting is in order.

Rutting bucks often scent-check all the exit routes by crossing them in perpendicular fashion some distance from the feeding area. The trails they use can be quite faint, but generally are dotted with rubs or a scrape or two showing up at the juncture of the buck run and the doe exit trails. This, too, is a good spot for a tree stand ambush, or you can elect to still-hunt downwind of the buck route. Either way, a doe-in-heat bleat followed by a few tending buck grunts can help tip the odds in your favor.

332

Go slowly and keep your eyes peeled, being sure not to jump any resting deer. Bucks and does sometimes bed down together on an open hillside or a finger of brush, and if you're careful you might just catch them flat-footed in repose.

333

You can also set up along a doe exit trail or where several doe trails converge along a ridgeline, or disappear into a swamp or clear-cut. If you tried these strategies during the pre-rut you would only see young bucks, but during the peak of the rut, hunting doe feeding areas is a great tactic for mature bucks.

334

Bucks know which trails the does prefer, as evidenced by rubs and scrape lines. When buck sign and doe sign overlap during the peak of the rut, you have all the makings for a hot stand site. Be very careful in your approach, however, especially if you plan to set up near the primary feeding site. The last thing you want to do is spook the does in the early-morning light.

335

A bedded doe can also signify that she is near estrous, but not quite ready to breed. (She beds down to keep an aggressive buck at bay.) Once again, it's not uncommon for several bucks to be standing nearby when a doe is near estrous. If you add a few yearling tending buck grunts or emit some "buck clicking" with your grunt tube, an approaching buck, especially if he's at least two years old and sexually experienced, may just rush right in. Why? He might "think" there's another buck in attendance and as soon as the doe stands up, this other buck is going to breed her—unless he gets there first!

336

Bowhunting doe feeding areas and doe travel routes are both good strategies for the peak of the rut. Most of the action is generally early in the morning, and secondarily late in the afternoon.

337

My favorite tactic in the peak of the rut is to wait for a cold front and then still-hunt the bedding area starting at first light. Rubber boots and a drag-rag soaked with estrous doe urine or a fox cover-up scent helps minimize my human odor. As with feeding areas, be aware that a rutting buck can show up at any time, so circling back and forth and all around a bedding area is a good tactic.

During the rut, unbred does are always looking for bucks!

As the pre-rut fades into memory, an estrous doe bleat—either alone or followed by a series of tending buck grunts—might just bring a passing buck into range.

338

A rutting buck can show up to investigate a known bedding area at any time of the day, making this location the odds-on favorite for the peak of the rut. The only problem here is that it's very easy to spook a matriarchal doe, causing the family group to abandon the site for several days or a week.

339

If you see a mature doe with a buck in tow, and they're working their way past you just out of range, try a lost fawn bleat to appeal to the doe's maternal instincts, followed by both a doe-in-heat bleat and a tending buck grunt. This strategy mimics those times when a doe abandons her fawn while being bred by a buck in attendance.

340

If you prefer to bow hunt from a tree stand, then consider using a drag-rag soaked in doe-in-heat urine and cross the major entrance and exit trails on the way to your stand. Set up just outside the doe bedding area on the downwind side of one of those trails, and remain alert.

341

Keep in mind that a rutting buck often follows a doe until she beds down outside the bedding area. One year I found nine bucks bedded down with one doe in a goldenrod field adjacent to a known bedding site.

342

As the rut heats up, bucks no longer respond to rattling sequences as readily as they did during the pre-rut. Nor can you depend on a response by mimicking a single contact grunt from another buck. But let a mature rutting buck hear a long drawn-out doe bleat, and he may very well lower his head and charge your position!

343

After a doe-in-heat bleat try adding a five-second series of staccato-like grunts imitating a yearling buck. This ruse may convince a rutting buck that a hot doe is nearby keeping company with a young amorous buck. An older and more mature buck will certainly feel the need to investigate.

Although trophy bucks lower their guard during the breeding season, the concept of "trophy" is often in the eyes of the beholder. This 6-point buck could still eat, but the tip of his rack had grown inside his mouth, making him a once-in-a-lifetime treasure.

344

Let's say you spy a lone mature buck obviously seeking estrous does. He takes a few steps, sniffs the air and then the ground while looking intently all around. What would be your vocalization of choice? Again, a long and drawn-out fawn bleat. Why? The key word is "mature." A young buck may pay little or no heed, but a mature buck knows that a fawn looking for its mother often means one thing: The doe is nearby being bred by another buck. That plaintive wail may prompt him to circle downwind and sneak in for a look.

345

Want to have some real fun? Add a moderately toned clicking buck call to the ruse. A mature buck recognizes that as the sounds a subordinate buck makes to a doe just prior to breeding. With any luck, the old buck will simply rush in to take over the breeding chores.

346

Let's say you see a mature doe being followed by a mature buck, both of which are about to pass out of range. She is obviously trying to elude him, probably because she is still a day or so from ovulating. The buck instinctively knows this and tries to keep his distance without running her off. What vocalization might you try? A doe contact grunt! Her behavior tells you she would like to dump her suitor, and one way for her to do this is to get him interested in another doe, possibly one closer to estrous. She will respond to your call, with the old boy in tow, in an effort to lose the buck by crossing trails with a second (or even a third!) female.

347

Here is another scenario. You're on your way to your stand, and suddenly a fat doe darts out of the brush in front of you, sees you and ducks back into the thick stuff. You then hear a series of grunts and watch as one, two and then three bucks break from the same cover, see you and scatter. A few moments later you hear noises and assume at least one of the bucks is circling around in an effort to relocate the hot doe.

What vocalization should you try? Actually, almost any whitetail rendition brings results, but an estrous doe bleat is your best option simply because that is what the bucks are looking for. Be ready to shoot before you call, however, as it will only take a second for a nearby buck to materialize in front of you.

348

Let's say you've seen plenty of deer since first light, including a monster buck that chased a doe past your stand 10 minutes earlier. Suddenly, you catch a buck yearling sneaking around where you saw the big buck. You aren't picky and would be proud to put your tag on this buck.

What call should you use? A moderately toned tending buck grunt. Why? That yearling is probably a satellite buck, hoping against hope to sneak in and breed the doe the big buck is pursuing. He knows his chances are slim, but when he hears your rendition of a young buck tending another doe, he might just creep in hoping to steal that estrous doe from a buck more his size.

Seeing such a trio of bucks will make you think it's your lucky day—if you can connect on one of them.

TRY A SNORT-WHEEZE

It's late in the day and you watch as a hot doe crosses an open field with a big-racked buck nose-to-tail behind her. You sense that breeding could take place soon. How can you get that buck to leave her and approach your crouched position?

Although you could try a deep-toned buck grunt, the vocalization of choice here is a snort-wheeze. Here's why: That mature buck knows he is about to breed, and he doesn't want any interference. At first he may try to usher her away, but if you're persistent, and maybe even close the distance a bit, he may very well try to run you off.

You'd better be ready to shoot before you call, because the action can be swift and furious.

WEARING BLAZE ORANGE EFFECTIVELY

Let's face the facts: Blaze orange helps prevent hunters from being mistaken for game and keeps them out of the line of fire. And if a hunter is lost or becomes sick in the field, a simple orange vest can also help search and rescue personnel locate him or her from the ground or from the air. Indeed, blaze orange has helped make hunting safer than fishing, canoeing and a wide range of popular contact sports.

Nonetheless, some hunters still refuse to wear blaze orange, whether mandated by law or not. They simply may be hunters who feel their chances of bagging a buck are poorer if they obey blaze-orange regulations.

Although biologists aren't sure how deer perceive color, especially hunter orange, plenty of anecdotal evidence suggests that deer see a hunter dressed head to toe in fluorescent orange before they see a hunter dressed from head to toe in modern camouflage.

How then can you remain safe, comply with the law and still get close to a whitetail deer? It's easier than you think!

349

Choose your outerwear carefully. Look for fabrics that are not shiny, such as plastic or vinyl, but rather brushed cotton or twill that have a dull finish and do not reflect as much light.

350

Consider 3-D or crinkle-cut clothing. These garments reflect even less light than a solid block of cotton or twill, and therefore distort the human form better. The wearer is even less likely to be seen by a wary buck.

351

Does your hunting garment have to be solid blaze orange? In some locales the answer is yes, but where it's legal, blaze orange camouflage—with its black blotches and squiggles printed on top of a solid blaze orange background— can go a long ways toward breaking up your human outline.

Stay safe! Always wear some orange when hunting with friends or in heavily populated regions.

Getting help with the drag makes a shorter day.

352

To break up your human form created by that solid block of blaze orange worn on your chest, back and shoulders, don an orange vest over a camo jacket. It will do the job nicely, especially if that jacket is cut to 3-D.

353

Deer are keen on picking out objects that move, and few colors accentuate movement as much as blaze orange, in part because it contrasts sharply with any natural background.

354

Blaze orange can also be used for a ribbon trail when you need to return later with help for the dragging chores.

355

You can mix and match various camouflage patterns. You do not need to be a slave to fashion, however. In fact, a hat, jacket, shirt and pants in different patterns combined with a solid or 3-D blaze orange vest can be very effective at breaking up the human outline.

356

Climb a tree, preferably a large-diameter specimen with lots of leaves and branches. Deer do look up, mind you, but they need a reason. As long as you're quiet, have the wind in your favor and don't move, you will remain undetected no matter how much blaze orange you are wearing or where it is on your body.

357

Where legal, consider taking your blaze orange vest off and hanging it in a nearby branch once you climb aloft. This will alert other hunters to your position and still allow you to hunt in full camo. Or you can wrap the trunk several times with flagging tape. This tape is designed to be seen from a full 360 degrees, offering you even better protection than just a blaze orange vest, which is always partially hidden behind the trunk. Be sure the flagging tape is tied securely to the tree. Loose ends that flap and snap in the wind will most certainly attract any passing buck's attention.

The right pattern on your camo pants make you blend in with the leaf-strewn forest floor.

358

If you don't want to get into a tree stand, sit down next to a log or pile of stones, or crawl into a blow-down to help break up your human outline. You can also sit behind a large-diameter tree, not in front of it, or crouch low in a creek bed and peer over the top.

359

Even in areas where blaze orange is not mandatory, donning a blaze orange hat or vest is a good idea whenever you're walking in and out of the woods. You don't want to be mistaken for a whitetail trying to sneak past a concealed hunter.

360

There will be times when you do want everybody to see you wearing blaze orange—such as when you're carrying a deer decoy or setting one up in the field, or when you're trailing a wounded deer or dragging a tagged one back to camp. This is when you want your blaze orange cap and gloves to accentuate your body movements.

361

Even in states with high compliance rates, there are 5 to 10 percent of hunters who do not wear the required amount of blaze orange as prescribed by law. Some are poachers and trespassers while others simply don't believe in the sanity of the law. Their actions pose a substantial safety risk to all deer hunters. Why? If wearing blaze orange is mandatory, some hunters will believe that if it moves and is not wearing blaze orange, it must be a deer. The lesson is clear: Be safe! Wear some orange.

STILL-HUNTING

Still-hunting is both an art and a science. There are, of course, more efficient ways to harvest a buck, but none offer the deer hunter more pride and sense of accomplishment than still-hunting. These tips cannot guarantee you success, as there is no magic formula to bagging a buck. I can, however, guarantee you a special feeling when you pit your woodsmanship against that of a trophy buck this fall—and win!

Camouflage Clothing

362

Use total camouflage. That means all outer clothing, exposed skin and equipment must be dulled with earth-tone colors—unless you're hunting in the snow.

363

Use a cold cream–based camouflage cream to cover your entire face including ears, neck, forehead and eyelids. A camo handkerchief also covers your neck and helps keep you warm when temperatures dip below freezing.

364

Avoid wearing head nets because they invariably obscure your peripheral vision, muffle woodland sounds and impair your ability to detect subtle changes in wind direction.

365

Try this simple experiment to see how important it is to keep your hands covered. Have a buddy stand in the woods just on the edge of your vision, and first wave a gloved hand and then a bare hand in your direction. The bare hand stands out like a neon light!

Do you want to get the drop on a racked buck from the ground? Then look like you're part of the forest.

366

Learn to mix and match your camo for ideal concealment in a variety of situations. A good rule of thumb is to match your upper body with what's above the forest floor, and your lower body to what is on the forest floor.

367

Be sure to inspect your equipment carefully. White lettering on bow limbs, for example, is a no-no, as is a clear plastic pin guard. Why? They both stick out like flashlights in the dark. The solution is to spray paint over the "dead-give-away" lettering and all shiny surfaces on your bow, and either paint or replace that pin guard.

368

Don't overlook your arrow's fletching. Bright, contrasting colors are designed to help you find your arrow after the shot, but they're detrimental when they interfere with a shooting opportunity. A quiver full of brightly fletched arrows can sometimes spook a buck faster than a fluttering white handkerchief. If it's important for you to pinpoint the entry point of your broadhead, an acceptable compromise would be a light-colored cock feather or fluorescent nocks.

369

Nix the back quivers and hip quivers, and opt for a bow quiver instead. Why? The former two tend to be bulky and noisy in the brush. They are also another "dead give-away" to your position.

It's a must to have quiet equipment. And, if your outerwear squeaks or scratches when you drag a fingernail across the garment, it will most certainly give you away while hunting in the thick stuff.

Sounds of Silence

370

Brushed cotton is relatively quiet, as are products such as Polartuff, but wool is best.

371

What about footwear? Thin-soled boots with rippled soles help you feel the forest floor, but they're also slippery on wet surfaces. Heavy-duty lug soles offer good traction and protect your feet from sharp stones, but they don't allow you to feel twigs and other debris littering the ground. For still-hunting I use the Air Bob or Air Grip sole. Its main features are hollow black nipples that "bob" up and down as you walk, giving you incredible traction and good sensitivity.

372

Deer can easily tell the difference between a human walking in the woods, and a forest animal searching for food. How? A man seems to move about with a destination in mind. Instead of marching purposely through the woods, move about like a feeding deer. Their muted steps coupled with a stop-and-go tempo do not disturb forest residents.

373

Stick to the shadows and skirt the edges as you move, and never, never cross an opening in plain sight. Don't walk on the flat of a ridge either, but rather just below the crest. Your goal is to see what's ahead of you without being seen yourself.

If your outerwear squeaks or scratches when you drag a fingernail across the garment, it will most certainly give you away while hunting in the thick stuff. This is especially true of rain gear and some hunter-orange clothing.

Drinking may be enough diversion to let you get away with a little noise as you approach.

When still-hunting, don't look on the ground for deer sign until you're sure there are no deer in the immediate vicinity.

Loose-hanging binoculars can cause noise and movement problems; be sure yours are secured.

374

When in doubt about what path to follow, pretend there is a bedded buck just up ahead. Then think about how you can sneak up on him undetected. If you choose to approach along the edge of the swamp, use the alders as cover. If you must step into the water to mask your forward progress, then do so without sloshing!

375

Practice sneaking about with your eyes off the ground. Novices often spend too much time scanning the ground for deer sign, and not enough time looking up ahead in the brush for deer. This is a learned skill. Start by glancing on the ground for a spot to put your feet for the next two or three steps, and then without looking down again, take those steps while your eyes are searching each new vista for a leg or antler of a buck.

376

Follow this rule of thumb: spend 10 seconds of every minute looking on the ground, and 50 seconds of every minute looking up ahead for deer—any less and you're wasting your time.

377

If something odd or out of place catches your eye, don't move until you can identify it. It may just be the antler tine of a bedded buck facing away from you or the laid-back ear of a doe tending her fawn.

378

Leave the inexpensive and mini binoculars home; you need a quality pair of mid-sized glasses for still-hunting. The minis don't have the field of view or the light-gathering ability to help you locate bucks when they're most likely to be on the move—early morning and late evening.

379

Look for deer with your ears, too—they are noisy animals! The "urp-urp-urp" of a buck tending a doe is an obvious example, but deer make other noises as they go about their business. They "chomp-chomp" on apples and acorns, jump over barbed-wire fences causing a "twang, twang" and "splash" their way across streams. They "snip-snip-snip" off the tops of goldenrod plants and go "clackety-clack, clackety-clack" when they cross over a stone wall.

Scent Control

380

Knowing your hunting turf well helps control human odor. How? You'll no longer be spreading your odor to the four winds as you wander aimlessly about the woods in search of your quarry. Instead, you'll be stalking downwind or crosswind of known concentrations of deer.

381

Avoid hunting downwind even if you're wearing clean clothes and cover scents to camouflage your human stench.

Topographical maps, aerial photographs and plenty of shoe leather soon get you on intimate terms with your whitetail hot spot.

Use bottled talcum powder, a butane lighter or a feather tied to your bow or rifle to help you keep tabs on wind direction. An experienced still-hunter can often feel the subtle changes on his or her exposed skin and then react accordingly.

382

Carry maps with you during the off-season and study them in the field in preparation for both archery and firearm seasons.

383

Can you ever hunt with the wind to your back? Yes. You can always confidently still-hunt the tops of ravines or edges of cornfields with the wind behind you, because your scent will be drifting away from any probable concentrations of deer.

384

Pay constant attention to changes in wind direction by observing the swaying of leaves and plant stems in front of you, or the thread you have tied to your bow for just such a reason.

385

To catch a buck resting in his bed, work crosswind through known bedding areas. Remember, a buck usually beds on a ridge or along the edge of thick cover facing downwind. If you sneak along

with the wind in your face, he'll undoubtedly see you first and be long gone before you can work yourself into bow range.

386

Should you bathe regularly or wear cover scents? Yes. The less human scent in the air, the better. After all, do you want a buck to sneak back around you because he curiously whiffed a few molecules of vanilla or estrous doe urine, or run into the next valley to avoid gagging?

For best results, use scent-free or rubber gloves on foot pads when laying down a scent trail or applying cover-up scents.

387

One of the best ways to catch a rutting buck flat-footed is to play the wind as he does. He works crosswind in an effort to scent-check as many does as possible. In turn, you work crosswind, and catch him in the act.

388

Tow a drag-rag or wear scent pads on your feet soaked with urine from animals common to the area, such as fox, coyote, raccoon or skunk to help keep your still-hunting route from becoming a human scent trail. A glove soaked in urine can help keep your scent off low-hanging branches as you pass through the thick stuff.

How Fast is Too Fast?

389

If the rut is in full swing, sneaking along the edge of a feeding area known to be frequented by family groups of does and fawns might be a good tactic at any time of the day. Still-hunting slowly along the edge of a buck's bedding area when he is more likely to be out chasing the does, however, is not likely to produce much action—unless the thicket is also home to a herd of does and fawns!

390

If you happen to snap a twig or trip over a branch while still-hunting, use a fawn bleat. Young deer are always playing and crashing into things, and a few soft mews will relax any nearby deer.

You're moving too fast if all you see are white "flags" bouncing along in front of you.

391

Don't waste your time along a creek bottom or along the edge of a field if there's no fresh deer sign nearby. In fact, nothing ruins a future still-hunter faster than to spend the day crawling through the woods at a snail's pace and not see a deer. You need to still-hunt where deer habitually frequent if you expect to fill a tag.

392

If you are catching small game off guard, like foxes, coons and ruffed grouse, than you are probably moving at an acceptable speed, you are just hunting the wrong area at the wrong time of the day or period of the rut.

393

Jeff Grab knows when to sneak-and-peek. "Even if there is plenty of sign underfoot, that does not mean you should immediately begin slipping in and out of the shadows looking for deer. There may be a plethora of tracks and rubs along the edge of a cut corn lot, for example, but it would be folly for you to still-hunt here at high noon early in the season. The chances of you happening upon a buck then are nil. It would be just as foolish to skip past a known bedding area late in the evening. Going too fast then surely lessens your chances of a sighting."

394

Storm fronts are good days to be afield, in part because the howling winds, rustling leaves and swaying vegetation tend to mask your forward progress, thus allowing you to sneak around a bit faster than you normally would. You are simply less likely to be seen, heard or scented during stormy weather.

395

Nothing slows a still-hunter down faster than crunchy leaves or dry, brittle branches littering the forest floor. When ground conditions are not optimal, choose a different route, such as a cart road or fence row; you can wait until it rains or until the sun melts the morning frost and dampens the forest debris; or you can abandon the area until ground conditions are more favorable. Finally, you can take the debris-riddled route, but plan on only sneaking forward during prime time at 10 yards (9 m) an hour. And you better make it good because if there's a buck nearby, you'll probably only get away with it once.

Moment of Truth

396

When you catch an undisturbed buck flat-footed, immediately drop to one knee. If you can do so next to a log, a tree trunk or a bush, so much the better. Your goal is to mask your human form. No longer are you a two-legged creature standing nearly 6 feet (1.8 m) off the ground—a creature deer seem to instinctively fear. Instead, you're a dark stump or a mound of earth on the forest floor. You're something that belongs there—and nothing more.

Some hunters think it's reckless to still-hunt in crunchy leaves, but experienced still-hunters can always come up with a strategy to overcome this challenge.

397

Without taking your eyes off exactly where you want to shoot the deer, nock an arrow. Only a fool still-hunts with a nocked broadhead, so you must extract an arrow without banging the shaft against the hood of the quiver, or slapping it against the sight bracket or riser of the bow.

398

Timing is crucial when coming to full draw. You must wait for the buck to lower his head, step behind a tree or simply look away. Even if he catches you making the move, the buck often hesitates a second or two before bolting simply because he doesn't know what you are. And a second is all it takes.

399

Immediately after the shot, mark your shooting location with a strip of surveyor's tape. This allows you to return to that exact spot in case you can't find blood or your arrow.

400

First learn to still-hunt with archery tackle, and then apply those principles to still-hunting with a firearm. There is nothing, and I mean nothing, deadlier in the deer woods than a still-hunter who has traded his bow for a carbine.

Knowing exactly when to come to full draw is often based on experience; sometimes you just "feel" when it's right.

SNOW-TRACKING MATURE BUCKS

Tracking a buck in the snow and then shooting him is one tough job. It's certainly more difficult than ambushing driven deer or bushwhacking an unsuspecting buck from an elevated tree stand. Indeed, snow-tracking trophy bucks successfully is seen by many as the epitome of woodsmanship.

401

One of the best times to follow a buck's trail is during the rut at the tail end of a snowstorm, when new snow is no more than 6 inches (15 cm) deep. Family groups of does and fawns are still bedded, but the bucks are up and about looking for a doe near estrous as soon as they sense the storm is waning. You'll be able to age their tracks very easily if the snow is still falling, as any deer tracks you come across will cover up quickly with the last vestiges of the storm.

402

In wilderness areas, a mature buck outweighs the average doe by 100 to over 200 pounds (45 to 90 kg). This explains why a mature buck's track is bigger than that of a doe. If the earth is soft under the snow, his track will be splayed and his toes point outward, with his rear feet sinking deeper into the earth than a lighter, younger buck—mature bucks have bigger butts. His stride will also be longer, and because of his barrel chest, his trail in the snow will be wider than that of a doe, at least 6 inches (15 cm) to the left and right of the median. Rutting bucks also seem to drag their front feet a bit, probably to conserve energy, but after the snow reaches 6 inches (15 cm) or so, both bucks and does drag their feet.

Bucks will be out looking for estrous does as soon as the snowstorm shows signs of letting up. Get out there!

403

Still not sure how old the track is? Stomp your foot down in the snow next to the deer track, and study the differences. If both tracks are fresh, the edges and overall form should be similar in appearance.

404

It takes a few days for deer to get used to having snow on the ground. They "think" you can't see them even though their dark coats silhouette them against the white. Thus, the season's first snowfall is also one of the best times to track down a buck. Be in the woods just as the storm is letting up.

405

Look for pointed and elongated tracks with the dew claws set deep. These are almost always made by a buck, although a big doe can fool you now and then. Doe tracks are generally smaller and quite dainty.

406

If you backtrack a morning trail, you may discover where that buck was feeding in the wee hours before dawn. If you backtrack an evening trail, you may find where that buck has been bedding. Notice that a buck's evening and morning trails are generally one-way streets.

407

Does usually bed in family groups of does, yearlings and fawns as demonstrated by the number and size of the deer beds. A buck's bed is undoubtedly larger than that of a doe, and he usually beds alone.

Sometimes you can learn more by backtracking a buck. On evening trails, take a compass bearing and compare it to a topo map. It might give you a few clues about where the buck was bedding.

FOLLOW THE HOT DOE

One snowy autumn morning I came across three sets of large tracks weaving back and forth across a trail obviously laid down by a doe and two small fawns. I decided to give chase, believing I had three good bucks in front of me. I followed the tracks off a hardwood ridge and down into a swamp. Suddenly, I jumped the deer, and then watched in disbelief as first one, two and then three racked bucks ran back up the hill in front of me without offering a clear shot.

Dejected, I pondered my choices. At first, I wanted to continue the chase, but then I realized the bucks were after a hot doe, and if not pursued they would eventually circle around in an effort to hook back up with her.

I followed the doe and her fawns along the creek bed, careful not to disturb them. Twenty minutes later I heard two bucks grunting as they came back off the hardwood ridges. When the bigger of the two 8-pointers recklessly crossed the creek in search of the hot doe, I slugged him at 50 yards (45 m) with my 12-gauge Ithaca Deerslayer, dropping him dead in his tracks.

Amazingly, after completing the field-dressing chores, I watched as the other 8-pointer and a 10-pointer picked up the trail of the hot doe and continued their pursuit along the creek bed completely oblivious to my presence.

What do you think?

How do you know the buck is a 200-pounder (90 kg)? If your fist doesn't cover the spoor and it measures over 3 inches (7.5 cm) in width, then it's probably a 4½-year-old buck.

Jim Glidden, one of the founding fathers of the New Hampshire Skull and Antler Trophy Club with fifteen 200-pounders to his credit, told me, "You can look at the size of the track, but that can be deceiving.

"Over the years I have learned that under normal walking conditions a 200-pound mature buck has at least a two-foot stride. I actually measure the stride when I am on the trail, from the tip of the front hoof print to the heel of the rear hoof print. If the stride is 23½ to 24 inches (60 to 61 cm), the buck will only weigh 190 pounds (85 kg) dressed."

Charles Foote is an official measurer for the New Hampshire Skull and Antler Trophy Club and an avid snow tracker with nine 200-pounders (90 kg) on the wall.

He says, "You can help narrow your search for a trophy buck by looking for tracks in places you would expect a big buck to be. Natural bottlenecks are always a good starting point. I routinely find big tracks on beaver dams, for example, and inside saddles."

410

As you follow the trail, there will be other hints as to the sex of the deer. Obviously, new rubs and freshened scrapes are giveaways, but often it is the behavior that tells you that you're on the trail of a buck. A doe seems to wander about aimlessly, whereas a buck in the rut leaves a trail that appears straight and purposeful, even businesslike in fashion, as he moves through the woods from one concentration of does to the next in his seemingly endless search for a doe in heat.

411

A rutting buck stops to sniff-test each deer track he crosses, and if he has a trophy rack he leaves antler impressions in the snow during the process. Now you know how wide his rack is and maybe how many points it has, too.

412

Bucks also dribble urine and sprinkle deer pellets as they walk, whereas does generally stop to urinate and defecate.

413

Jim Massett, former president of the New York State Big Buck Club and die-hard snow tracker, can sex a deer trail just by looking at the urine stain the in the snow. As he tells it, a doe squats to urinate, leaving a stain dead center between her back legs. A buck, however, whose sheathed penis is positioned similar to that of a dog, urinates left or right and a bit forward of dead center.

414

Massett also correctly guessed the inside spread of a buck he was tracking one snowy day by simply measuring the distance between two trees the buck tried but could not walk between!

415

Should you only follow a buck's trail? "No," says Vermont deer expert Jeff Grab. "A doe's trail may also lead you to other concentrations of deer, including a racked buck. Besides, any doe that is up and about by herself is probably near estrous, and thus worth keeping an eye on."

416

Get a quick sense of where the tracks are going, and then as you move forward scour the area ahead for an antler beam or the flash of a tail. There will be plenty of time to examine the details of the trail once you're sure the buck is not up ahead or off to one side staring back at you. If you're not spending 90 percent of your time looking for the buck, then he's likely going to give you the slip. A quality pair of binoculars are a valuable asset.

417

While on the trail, never cross an opening without first glassing the far side for deer or evidence of deer activity in the snow. Remember, you can see farther in the woods with snow on the ground, and so can the deer.

Look for antler impressions in the snow whenever you come across the intersection of two deer trails.

Deep snow makes tracking a whole different challenge.

Many varieties of snow camo clothing work well in the field.

418

What should you do if you spook a buck? At first, absolutely nothing. Let the buck get away and calm down. Then after 20 minutes or so, continue trailing him. You can see that he bolted for 100 yards (91 m) or so, taking 25- to 30-foot (7.6 to 9 m) leaps before stopping behind heavy cover to check his backtrail for several minutes and then bolting again. Once he is assured you aren't after him, he'll eventually slow down and maybe even start looking to bed-up.

419

How fast should you move when tracking? That really depends on the buck. The rule of thumb is to match pace with the buck. If he's running, then you can move right along, but once he slows down to a trot and then a walk, you have to slow down, too. If he's stopping near blow-downs or in heavy cover to check his backtrail, and then radically changing direction of travel, it gets tricky. You must slow down now to a crawl and even circle around downwind, as he might be bedded just up ahead looking back on his trail.

420

"If the buck starts zigzagging he might have found a doe, or he is getting ready to bed down," says avid snow tracker Gene "Mickey" Meier, a retired Lieutenant in the New Hampshire State Police. "Break off the trail and make a circle. If you don't cut his track, get the wind in your favor and continue looking for him."

421

A common mistake snow-trackers make is walking right in the buck's tracks. If you lose the trail in the brush, you might need to go back to unravel the direction of travel. This can be especially difficult if the trail leads you through a feeding area such as an abandoned apple orchard or hardwood ridge littered with acorns and beechnuts. If you are following a mature buck, however, his tracks, gait and purposeful demeanor should help keep you from straying off course.

ON THE WATER

One of the secrets to tagging a good buck is to sneak in and out of his core area without disturbing him. After all, once a mature buck knows you are after him, he can be almost impossible to kill.

One of the most overlooked tactics is to utilize one of man's oldest inventions—the canoe. Indeed, when it comes to locating a big buck, and then getting in and out unnoticed, nothing beats paddling around in one of these sneaky crafts.

Once the darling of the hunting world, aluminum has since given way to space-age materials and computer-enhanced designs.

422

If you're thinking about purchasing an aluminum canoe, remember that they are shiny and need constant painting to eliminate glare. To reduce the noise potential, be sure to add carpet.

423

Polyethylene canoes are sensitive to ultraviolet light. They need storage under cover, and are really irreparable.

424

Fiberglass canoes are a good choice for slow-moving waters. You can easily poke a hole, so avoid rapids unless you are experienced.

425

Kevlar canoes are another good choice for slow-moving waters, but quite expensive. Skip this type if you're not ready to make repairs.

426

Royalex composite crafts don't readily transmit heat or cold, which is a big plus on an ice-choked stream in November. Try this type if you're a late-season hunter. You can usually purchse a used one at half the price of new in the fall.

Accessories

427

Your new canoe is not yet a deer-hunting tool, however. First, it is generally illegal, and certainly unwise, to paddle anywhere without personal flotation on board. Be sure you wear it if you're paddling in the dark, in unknown waters, in rain-swollen creeks or if there are any obstacles in the water. It takes only a second to slide up on a submerged log or flip a canoe over in rough water. And I can tell you from personal experience that ice-swollen waters are v-e-r-y c-o-l-d. When in doubt, scout the water up ahead before committing yourself to an unknown stretch of turbulence.

428

Store at least one extra set of dry clothing, including boots plus rain gear, waterproof matches, topo map, compass and a flashlight in a waterproof bag.

The core of a composite canoe is foam that not only stiffens but also silences the boat, making it the quietest canoe on the market.

CANOE CHOICES

Aluminum canoes have a keel that hangs down almost a full inch (2.5 cm). If you hang up on an underwater object in midstream, the canoe stops and then pivots on the point, making it very difficult to maneuver. Instead of flexing and sliding over objects, they tend to swing about in the current and wrap themselves around the object.

Polyethylene canoes are made of inexpensive plastic. They are, however, excessively heavy, too heavy in fact to easily paddle, load and unload when you are alone.

Fiberglass canoes are a bit lighter than the polyethylene models, but they're also noisier in the riffles. Shiny surfaces need to be sanded and camouflaged.

Kevlar canoes are also noisy over rocks but lighter in weight than most fiberglass canoes. They are repaintable but not maintenance-free.

Composite crafts are your best all-around choice for float-hunting whitetails. They are self-healing; you can drive a nail or a sharp stick through the hull, and the foam simply closes up around the hole. The inner and outer layers are made of durable vinyl that is also U-V resistant. The next two layers are ABS plastic, which gives the canoe structure. They maneuver well and are very stable.

429

Be sure to install bow and stern lines, and then get in the habit of tying the craft to an object onshore each time you disembark—especially during periods of heavy rain. It can be a long, long walk to your vehicle if you and your ride get separated!

430

Paddle quietly. You lose the advantage offered by an inconspicuous approach if you splash water or hit the hull with your paddle. I paddle slowly and use a gloved hand to keep the handle from whacking the side of my canoe. It also doesn't hurt to pad the gunnels and thwarts with an old blanket while you're learning.

431

Canoes are thought of primarily as a big woods tool, to which they are ideally suited. But don't overlook paddling through active farmland. Big bucks often hide along brush-lined banks and are generally oblivious to your approach.

432

Carry plenty of potable water with you, as a day afloat can easily leave you dehydrated. Don't be tempted to drink from the river or stream if you become thirsty—it may not be safe.

433

Make sure you have your rifle ready at all times. The deer are most likely going to be very close, and you won't have much time to shoot before they run into the brush.

Waterproof as much gear as feasible before shoving off. If you are crossing a large body of water, tie your firearm to one of the supports just in case.

Remember to use potable water for cooking.

Getting the drop on backwater bucks may entail short, two-person drives.

AVOID BEAVER FEVER

Many big woods hunters have drank "mountain dew" and then returned home only to become quite ill with abdominal cramps, persistent watery diarrhea, foul-smelling gas, loss of appetite, vomiting, fever, chills and a general feeling of weakness. The culprit is *Giardia lamblia*, or "beaver fever" as it is more commonly called, and I'm told it can make you wish you never went to the mountains.

The disease has a two-week incubation period and is usually acquired by drinking contaminated water—water in which infected animals like muskrats, raccoons, dogs and beavers have defecated. *Giardia* is treatable, but as with many ailments, prevention is less costly and more desirable.

The easiest way to disinfect your drinking water is to boil it for 10 minutes plus 1 minute for each 1,000 feet (305 m) above sea level. Commercial remedies are also available, but you have to remember to bring them and use them religiously.

434

When floating down a river, keep gun safety in mind. Only the hunter sitting in the bow should be allowed to shoot from the canoe. The job of the person in the stern is to steer the canoe downstream in such a manner as to avoid underwater snags, rocks and the like, while at the same time choosing a route that offers the person in the bow the best shooting opportunity.

435

Carry an extra paddle. You may have to let your primary paddle slip into the current rather than risk banging it around inside the canoe when a buck suddenly materializes.

One of the joys of hunting from a canoe is "dragging" your trophy back to camp.

Hunting Strategies

436

Leave one guy off upstream, and then have the other paddler beach the canoe downstream ¼ mile (0.4 km) or so. One hunter can still-hunt toward the canoe or both hunters can walk slowly toward each other.

437

Pay close attention to brushy gullies and the confluence of smaller streams. If you see a buck and can't get a shot off, don't panic. Simply take note of the wind and sneak back.

438

Watch for bedded deer, especially on the bends and anywhere a hardwood ridge juts down to the edge of the water. A solitary buck often stays bedded and watches you pass, so does a buck bedded down with a doe.

439

Set up an ambush near a water crossing. Better yet, backtrack the trail in both directions, and you might discover a new bedding area or food source.

440

Shooting from a canoe is not as easy as it would seem, especially on a flowing river. It's like shooting at a moving target, only in reverse. Instead of a stationary hunter shooting at a walking or running buck, the buck is stationary and the hunter is on the move, floating first toward the animal and then away. That's why the paddler in the stern is so important. You must point the canoe at the deer whenever possible, even it means floating sideways or backward for a spell. A forked stick can be an asset under these circumstances.

441

Check your topo map, pull the canoe onto shore near one of those hardwood ridges or gentle slopes leading down to the water and try still-hunting or blind calling for a couple of hours. This is a great way to learn new country, one section at a time.

442

Back eddies, adjacent swamps, hummocks and river bends in wilderness areas, and wooded glens in farm country are all good places to try a grunt tube or a set of rattling horns. Set up downwind or crosswind with the water to your back.

Chapter 4

THE LATE SEASON

The late season generally gives bowhunters and black powder enthusiasts one more chance to fill a buck tag. To be successful now, you must first understand the effects of testosterone and how bucks behave during the post-rut period. Then you must develop new strategies to help you deal with skittish bucks, hunting in the snow, and cold weather. Finally, when the buck season closes, it is time to start scouting for next season.

Researchers tell us that about three-fourths of the available does are usually bred during the two-week peak of the rut. During this period the does and fawns are very hungry, and they spend a great deal of their time on the move, eating. This not only keeps their energy levels high, but also makes them more visible to roaming bucks.

Mature bucks, however, don't seem as hungry as the does, probably due in part to their extraordinarily high testosterone levels. They also don't take the time to eat, browsing only once in a while, for fear that another buck will horn in on some of the breeding action. Indeed, they have one thing on their minds now, and that is finding estrous does and then mating with them.

As the rut tails off, bucks zero in on the last estrous does, does that in many cases have not been as readily available. The family groups of does and fawns in crop fields and open meadows are now feeding alone. They're not being harassed by rutting bucks simply because they've all been bred. This is the beginning of the post-rut period when the number of buck sightings drops significantly, and we start asking ourselves "where have all the bucks gone?"

443

Your first option is to return to those primary scrapes and scrape lines that were hot during the pre-rut. Rutting bucks freshen these scrapes, scrapes that have been dormant for several weeks, and start checking their status for one last doe.

Sometimes the bucks bed down nearby and wait for a doe to wander by. Ironically, sometimes does that have yet to be bred seek out these freshened scrapes and reworked scrape lines in an effort to contact a mature buck.

444

As the effects of testosterone fade, bucks will begin to move about more freely. The secret to locating a buck now is food.

445

Still-hunting is your odds-on most productive tactic now. Look for bucks to be resting in thick tangles of brush, overgrown meadows, steep slopes, mountaintops, humps in swamps and the heads of deep ravines.

446

Study topo maps, and look for old apple orchards, vineyards and farmlands that are off the beaten path as well as those expansive lowland edges along rivers, lakes and swamps that can attract hungry deer. Orchards and vineyards show up as several parallel rows of squiggly circles, whereas hidden agricultural fields often lie beyond roads and on the far side of large woodlots.

After 7 to 10 days, the rut is finally over, and the bucks go into seclusion.

Snow can pile up during the late black powder and archery seasons. Modern snowshoes can get you in and out of the deer woods with minimal effort. I keep a pair in my truck all season long.

447

Look for terrain features that can protect deer during the fall fusillade as well as from the cold winds of December and January. Ravines, gullies and steep ridges should immediately come to mind, especially those that are adjacent to agricultural fields, large swamps, abandoned apple orchards and hardwood ridges known to be thick with hickory, beech and oak mast.

448

Deep snow may inhibit your access to any of these late-season feeding areas. If so, think outside the box. I once used snowshoes to get to a cornfield that was being visited regularly by nearly 20 deer. That field was more than 1 mile (1.6 km) from the nearest plowed road, offering deer both food and privacy. A nearby steep ravine offered additional cover and wind protection.

449

Still unable to find a sizable population of deer? After the first late-season snowfall, look for deer tracks where you wouldn't normally expect to find deer, and then follow the first set you locate. Invariably, those tracks lead to other deer tracks and then to a hitherto unknown late-season feeding area such as an oak ridge above a swamp or a windswept alfalfa lot.

450

A buck's main goal in the late season is to nourish himself after the rigors of the rut. However, a mature buck will perk right up if he believes there is a chance to mate once more with an estrous doe. A canister of estrous doe gel hung crosswind to your stand might just turn his head.

451

As the temperatures drop and winter sets in, expect deer to be more active during the middle of the day when it is the warmest.

452

On days of extreme cold, expect deer to stay out of the wind and seek nearby thermal cover where they stay until temperatures rise once more.

453

You may not see a lot of deer, or you could have 20 or so go thundering past you on any given outing. That's because deer gang up and then feed together in herds during the late season. The bucks will still be last to enter any feeding area.

454

Expect deer to congregate on south-facing hillsides. Still-hunt back and forth crosswind, and you might just catch a buck bedded facing downhill.

455

Bucks are plain tuckered out from the rigors of the rut, so they'll be bedding close by the food source. Therefore, set your stand closer to the food source than you normally would, being careful not to disturb any nearby bedded bucks. Make sure you approach your stand carefully and climb aloft quietly.

Be especially vigilant when erecting stands in the late season, since sound travels farther on clear, cold days.

A gathering call, such as a doe bleat or a fawn bleat, attracts family groups of does and fawns to your position, which in turn can attract any nearby bucks out trolling. Keep any rattling to a minimum. You can tickle the antlers, but don't mimic an active fight. Bucks will actually flee from a bloody-sounding fracas now.

458

If temperatures are frigid, try a canister call. It's easy to use; just turn the canister upside down and then right side up again to get a realistic b-a-a-a-t. A nice added feature is that these devices won't freeze up, since you don't need to breathe into them.

459

If you see an unusually large doe, look at the top of the head before you shoot. In many parts of the country, trophy bucks lose their headgear first, and the big doe you shoot during the late season could very well turn out to be the gigantic buck you saw last summer—sans antlers!

You can use natural habitat for a makeshift blind.

456

Set up a doe decoy in plain sight and upwind from your stand. It acts as a confidence decoy for the does and as an attractor for patrolling bucks. Be sure she is facing the direction you expect deer to approach from and that she is in range of your bow or muzzleloader.

KEEPING WARM

The longer you remain vigilant in the deer woods the better your chances of tagging a buck. But staying alert often means staying warm, not always an easy task when the temperatures dip below freezing. Indeed, when hunters get too cold they tend to stomp their feet and wave their arms like a wounded bird—activities that quickly tip-off nearby bucks to their presence.

Hunting all day in the cold can be a challenge in the late season. A daypack stuffed with a few essentials can keep you comfortable from dawn to dusk.

460

To upgrade your old hunting boots to subfreezing temperatures, add a pair or two of felt soles, available in most sporting goods stores. Boot bottoms are a major source of heat loss.

461

Wear an inner sock (anything but cotton) to wick moisture away from your feet, and at least one pair of wool or wool-blend socks. Never wear so many socks that they bind your feet or reduce circulation.

462

I carry at least one pair of dry socks and a pair of Gore-Tex waterproof socks in case I fall into a creek over the top of my boots. Simply pull the Gore-Tex socks over the dry wool socks, and your feet will stay warm and dry despite the wet boot.

Gathering around a fire on a cold day can lift the spirits.

463

Keep a pair of dark sunglasses in your fanny pack for those bright days afield. Sunshine reflecting off fresh snow can cause "snow blindness" and tire you out quickly. Keep in mind that your eyes use nearly 25 percent of your daily energy resources.

464

If your deer camp has electricity, dry your leather boots and liners each night with a commercial dryer. Don't put them near the fire, as this can cause the leather to split and crack. Re-apply waterproofing nightly.

465

If you're hunting a great distance from camp, carry an extra pair of liners in a fanny pack or daypack. If you must spend the night in the woods, these dry and sweat-free liners will help keep your feet from freezing. A piece of felt liner also makes a satisfactory fire starter.

466

Loose fitting wool mittens keep your hands warmer than a pair of tight leather gloves. However, if you prefer to hunt bare handed as I do, then a couple of chemical hand-warmers in each pocket keep your fingers nimble and ready for action. A couple of chemical hand-warmers stuffed in the bottom of each boot help keep your feet warm, too.

467

Your head and neck are major sources of heat loss. Wear a hat that covers your ears, and tie a bandana around your neck when hunting in subfreezing weather. A face mask also helps protect your exposed skin from frostbite.

468

Dress in layers to stay warm. Yet don't put on so many clothes they cut off circulation or stop you from moving about with ease.

469

A pair of loose-fitting wool pants held up with suspenders keeps you warmer than pants held in place with a belt cinched snugly around your waist. Suspenders help trap air without cutting off circulation.

470

Keep the tops of your boots laced snugly. This area is another potential major source of heat loss.

Keeping warm means staying alert. And staying alert is the ticket to seeing more deer.

471

To keep snow out of your boots and body heat in, wrap a length of rawhide around your pant leg, securing each pant leg to the outside top of your boot.

472

If you're hunting from a tree stand, sit on a thick cushion and place your feet on another. Use overstuffed boot warmers and a sleeping bag when the temperatures drop.

473

There is only one acceptable type of clothing in snow country—wool. Why? When wet, wool retains its insulating capabilities.

474

Still cold? Take this advice passed down to me from an old-timer: Carry a 6-foot (1.8 m) length of rope in your daypack, and when you feel a chill tie it around the nearest log and start dragging it. You'll warm up in no time!

Stay active during periods of freezing cold and you'll more likely remain alert.

HUNTING BUCKS IN THE SNOW

Hunting whitetails in the snow presents a unique set of problems for today's hunter. Not only must you stay warm, you must also spend considerably more time looking for deer. Often, they're no longer hanging around their old haunts. And once you find them, you have to figure out a way to put your tag on one. Late-season bucks are skittish!

475

Deer can easily smell acorns under a foot (30 cm) of snow. Don't dismiss areas around oak trees for a great late-season opportunity.

476

When it's snowing, snow camo is your most practical choice of outerwear, especially in 3-D. Choose a style with an attached hood. When pulled over your head, it breaks up the human outline more than any other piece of apparel.

477

Consider spray painting your gun or bow white for hunting the late season. If you are a real snow-country deer hunter, have back-up weapons pre-painted for late-season duty.

478

Picking up shed antlers can give you information about the area bucks. It can also be an excuse for getting out in the field in the off-season.

Monitoring beds and scrapes give you good information as to deer activity in your hungting area.

Consider becoming an official measurer for the Pope & Young Club or the Boone & Crockett record book.

479

Keep in mind that some commercial deer lures freeze once it is cold enough for snow to be on the ground. Many gels and pastes do not.

480

During snowstorms keep an eye on your arrow shafts and broadheads. Snow and ice can accumulate here, causing unpredictable arrow flight.

481

Because bowhunting in the snow and cold requires wearing bulkier clothing, consider dropping the poundage and lowering the draw length of your bow. You'll be able to come to full draw easier, and you won't be as likely to hit your arm with your bowstring.

482

Ever wonder how many bucks you walked by during a morning's hunt? Try this exercise, and see for yourself. Double back on your trail after an hour or two, and count the number of deer that crossed your tracks after you passed by!

POST-SEASON SCOUTING

Any deer hunter who bags a buck season after season will tell you that the key to success begins with post-season scouting. Begin your scouting excursions soon after the close of the late season, and do not worry about spooking deer as you move about your hunting turf. Your goal is to better understand the relationship between breeding areas and prefferred feeding and bedding sites. Remember: You are not hunting, but trying to get a handle on the local deer population—The Big Picture!

483

Visit local taxidermists, gun and archery shops, hunting clubs, and quiz rack scorers to learn where the bigger bucks are being shot. Often one county boasts the most buck kills while a second county has a lower deer kill, but a better big-buck take.

484

With the leaves down and maybe snow on the ground, search for terrain features that promote deer travel, such as gentle slopes that lead up and down hillsides, spurs and saddles between ridges, plateaus above farm fields and brush-choked ravines.

485

Watch for fresh late-season rubs the size of your fist. They could indicate a trophy buck survived the deer season.

486

Seek out natural bottlenecks along travel routes, and mark them on your map for future reference. This is a good time to build ground blinds. If you are a bowhunter, trim shooting lanes, depositing limbs away from the proposed stand site. Plan your approach carefully at this time, taking ground cover and prevailing winds into consideration.

Your goal is to learn how a buck can enter and leave his bedding area undetected, and what role the wind plays.

Some landowners have good reasons to keep hunters off their property. To prove you are a responsible hunter, stop and ask why before the season starts. You might just make a new friend.

487

The most promising logging roads are washed out or impassable in several places and overgrown with brush, whereas the roads least likely to lead you to previously unknown buck hangouts are located at trailheads. The presence of tire tracks and roadside trash should deter you from any further exploration.

488

Penetrate known and suspected buck bedding areas, looking for beds, rubs, drops as well as entrance and exit trails. Notice how close these safety zones are to agricultural fields in farm country, and old apple orchards, swamps, clear-cuts, and stands of mast in the big woods.

489

Don't be fooled by extra-large beds found near preferred late-season feeding locations. Mature bucks generally bed as close as they can to food supplies and in the thickest cover available during the cold winter months in part to save calories. As spring approaches, they retreat to more distant and safer locations.

490

Note the locations of all mast-producing trees, especially oak, beech, hickory and apple. Wet springs and summers can help mast grow, but late-spring frosts and dry summers can have a harmful effect on mast production, so plan on returning several times during the summer months for an update. You'll need binoculars to peer into the uppermost branches.

491

In wilderness areas, old logging roads can help you break up large sections for easier scouting. Follow them to see where they go. Remember that they make great still-hunting routes when dry leaves litter the forest floor, and should you get lost or turned around in the heat of the chase, they can help prevent you from spending an unwanted night under the stars.

492

In an effort to extend the boundaries of your hunting turf, scout adjacent parcels in a systematic fashion. Permission to trespass is often more easily granted in the dead of winter, which can lead to new friendships and expanded hunting opportunities. Pinpoint where deer "cross the line" from one parcel to the next, and then ask yourself why.

493

Topo maps can help you find hot spots in the big woods. Look for cart roads, jeep trails and old logging roads that seem to dead-end in the middle of nowhere. The presence of several "black boxes" around the end of the trail often indicate outbuildings from an old farmstead, complete with abandoned fields, apple trees and water—ideal habitat for racked bucks.

494

Traditional ash and rawhide snowshoes have long given way to the modern snowshoe. Now anyone can zip across deep snow with speed and agility.

A buck and doe together presents a certain challenge to your hunt!

WALK ON TOP

Do not let deep snows deter you from your mission. Unlike the ash and rawhide versions of yesterday, modern snowshoes are shorter, sleeker and more maneuverable, thanks in part to aluminum tubing framing, space-age bindings, solid abrasion-resistant decking and strategically positioned crampons. The end result is better stability or articulation when you're traversing along the edges of steep ravines or thick swamps.

Modern bindings fit snugly over any boot and, unlike the old rawhide bindings, don't stretch when wet. They're incredibly comfortable and help hold your foot in place all day long despite the temperature or changes in terrain. The better snowshoes are now left and right footed, allowing for even better foot control. You can put on a pair of snowshoes in seconds now, and leave them on all day long without further adjustment.

Even so, in the case of very deep snows, avoid yarding areas to help keep winter stress levels to a minimum.

495

Be on the lookout for evidence of other hunters during your scouting trips. If you know where another hunter is likely to be, you can plan alternative strategies for not only the bow season, but the regular firearm season as well. ATV trails, 4x4 tracks, shell casings, candy wrappers and of course human footprints should all tell you that you're not alone, as do tree stands, pull-up ropes, climbing pegs and scent bombs.

496

Look carefully for trail markers, such as orange ribbons, slashed tree trunks and reflective tape or thumb tacks, as well as conspicuous shooting lanes complete with piles of nearby brush. These often indicate an inexperienced hunter who is not familiar with the lay of the land. Compared with a more seasoned hunter, he or she is more likely to inadvertently interfere with your efforts.

497

Subfreezing temperatures can be an asset during your post-season scouting forays. Iced-over creeks, pond, lakes, cattail marshes, beaver dams and flooded timber all offer better access to big buck hideouts that can be easily and more thoroughly examined during the dead of winter. Look for deer beds, tracks, rubs, scrapes, droppings and major trails leading in and out of heavy cover, and start planning next season's ambush.

Finding sheds tells you lots of information about the herd in your area.

498

Look for humps and dry islands that would be otherwise difficult to locate during the early fall. These are often big buck sanctuaries during the gun season. You may find a rub or two on the island, but it is the presence of large-diameter deer droppings of varying ages that should get your heart pumping—they indicate a buck has probably been bedding there somewhat regularly.

499

In areas where deep snows are typical and in times when food and cover are scarce, deer travel more than 15 miles (24 km), sometimes 10 miles (16 km) in a single day, to traditional winter yarding sites. Fawns and rutting bucks weakened from the rigors of the rut are often the first to succumb to starvation. If you are a trophy hunter you may want to avoid these regions until a new fawn crop reaches maturity.

500

The temperature in a thick stand of conifers can be 10°F to 15°F (−12 to −9°C) warmer on a cold, sunny day than the temperature in a nearby cut corn lot. Factor in the wind chill, and you have a toasty hideaway for late-season deer.

501

BONUS TIP!
Get a kid interested in guns and hunting at an early age. If we don't, skateboards, the mall and electronic games will keep them away from the woods.

Hunting is a life-long sport. The best deer hunters start early, and get better at it with age.

ACKNOWLEDGMENTS

There have been many people over the years who have influenced my passion for deer hunting—some without knowing it. Like my grade school bus driver who slowed our yellow Blue Bird to a crawl so we could admire a sleek 6-point buck racing along a nearby creek. That memory is still vivid 50 years later.

And the unknown deaf kid who taught a 13-year-old the Morse code by first teaching me to listen, and later the undergraduate blind schoolmate who taught me to see clearly by using all my senses, not just my eyes, and for all the many schizophrenic patients I worked with in various psychiatric institutions who taught me how to communicate by using my brain and my heart.

And also my professors at Tulane University Graduate School of Social Work who helped me on the road to self-discovery by teaching me to first understand my emotions. How can you write and photograph effectively without knowing who you really are?

Indeed, I may not remember all their names, these people who walked briefly into my life, but they are now part of my eternal soul, and for that I am most grateful.

Thanks also goes to M.R. James who bought my first photograph for *Bowhunter Magazine*, and Lamar Underwood, the only man to sit in the editor's chair for *Field & Stream*, *Outdoor Life* and *Sports Afield*, who purchased my first feature article for Harris Publications.

Since then deer hunting editors like Pat Durkin, Danny Schmidt, Jim Schlender from *Deer & Deer Hunting*, Gerry Bethge and Nino Bosaz from *Whitetail Strategies*; Jay Strangis, Lee Hoots, Ben Moyer, Greg Tinsely, and Bob Robb from *Petersen's Hunting* and *Bowhunting*; Gordon Whittington from *North American Whitetail*, Mike Toth, Glenn Sapir and Dave Hurteau from *Field & Stream*, Frank Miniter from *Outdoor Life*, Mike Strandlund from *Bowhunting World*, and John Zent from the *American Hunter* have all helped me hone my skills as both an outdoor writer and photographer.

Sharing campfires with other professionals has always been a learning experience for me, so thanks Mike Bleech, Brad Herndon, Judd Cooney, Charles Alsheimer, Greg Miller, Ken Allen, Jeff Murray, Lon E. Lauber, Ted Nugent, Gary Clancy, Chris Kirby, Ray Eye, Joe Arterburn, Karen Valentine, Kathy Etling, Kathy Butt, Ron and Tess Jolly, Scott Bestul, Roper Green, Greg Chevalier, Bill Jordan, Cuz' Strickland, Mark Drury, Steven C. Cooke, Ed Dentry, Greg Gutschow, Michael Hanback, Dave Henderson, Mike Mattly, Mike Seymour, Lance Krueger, Mike Levy, Bob McNally, Wade Nolan, Bill Fargason, Tad Brown, Jeff Probst, Mike Raykovicz, Wayne Radley, Eddie Lee Rider, Jr., Joe Sadowski, Dr. Dave Samuel, Richard Sapp, Dwight Schuh, Dan Small, Toby Bridges, John Skrabo, Richard P.

Smith, Ron Spomer, Will Primos, Ernie Calandrelli, Tom Tietz, Bryce Towsely, Wayne Van Zwoll, Tony Zappia and Game Wardens Dick Thomas and Gid Hanggi.

My hunting buddies also deserve public recognition. They have worked tirelessly for me through many buck hunting seasons packing gear, setting up camp and posing for the camera. I got the credit line, but without them many of the articles would have never seen the inside pages of a hunting magazine.

Indeed, you saw their faces, time and time again, but never knew their names. So, thanks a lot John Grab, Jeff Grab, Andy St. Clair, Kaleb St. Clair, Will Edwards, Allen Miraglia, Mike Van Der Meid, Tracy Hodge, John Yates, Jim Poole, Wayne Merritt, Brannon Byrne, Jon Kayser, Joe Quinn, Bryan Quinn, Scott Staines, Dick Bamann, Jim Utterback, Steve Lamboy, Mark Eddy, Scott Smith, Mike Romano, Doug Turnbull, Dave Plant, Don Plant, Rick Plant, Brian Plant, Wayne Shorey, Matt Wettish, Steve Kowalczyk and Dr. Jeff Seitzinger.

Finally, in memoriam, two of my hunting buddies, Terry Kayser and Jack Smith, have passed.

"Hey fellas, keep a seat open next to the campfire for me, will ya? I can't wait to talk to you about the buck I saw yesterday, down by the beaver dam, it was...."

INDEX

A

Acorns, 19
Aerial photos, using, 7
Air rifles, 80
Aluminum canoes, 115, 116
Ambush sites
  early season, 85
  finding, 30, 31
  near bodies of water, 119
  for nocturnal bucks, 91
  number to choose, 11
  during peak of rut, 58, 87
Animal damage to tree stands, 38
Animal urine
  on clothing, 48, 106
  on drag along pads, 34
  non-rutting buck, 52
Antlers for rattling, 71
Apple blossoms, 8
Apples, 19
Arrows
  during snowstorms, 130
  spraying with scent eliminators, 40
Attractant scents
  in freezing weather, 130
  handling, 40
  in late season, 122–123
  placing, 41
  types to use, 57
ATV noise, 32

B

Batteries for trail cameras, 45
Beaver flows, importance of, 15, 58
Bedding areas
  abandoned farm fields, 21
  around mountain laurel, 21
  blow-downs, 20
  calling near, 61
  of does monitored by bucks, 16
  late pre-rut season and, 55
  during late season, 14, 123
  during peak of rut, 87, 94–95
  post-season inspection of, 132
  preferred by bucks, 8, 13, 14
  proximity to feeding locations, 90
  reasons for changing, 14
  during rut season, 23
  signs, 15

sizes of, 111
stone walls, 22
timber harvesting areas, 17
time of day used, 13
when storms approach, 17
during winter, 17
Beechnuts, 19
Binoculars, 104
Bipods, 80
Blind calling, 62, 63
Blow-downs, 20
Boots
  caring for, 126
  controlling human scent on, 39, 48
  height of, 47
  modifying for cold, 125, 126,
    127–128
  rubber, 11, 42, 47
  for still-hunting, 103
Bottlenecks, finding, 30
Bowhunters
  advantages of digital deer calls for, 70
  arcing shots, 76
  area to aim for, 29
  camouflaging equipment, 102
  estimating distances, 74–76
  peak of rut tips for, 94, 95
  practicing at ranges, 72
  rubs/rub lines tips for, 52
  shooting accuracy
  correcting problems, 74
  effect of leaves and brush on, 76
  guides for canting bow, 73
  position and, 30, 31
  preparing for shot, 61
  during snowstorms, 130
  still-hunting practice, 73, 74
  timing for full draw, 109
  tree stand tips for, 28–31, 52
  when not to take shot, 76
Bows
  during snowstorms, 130
  spraying with scent eliminators, 40
Breeding trails, locating, 85, 88
Brush removal, 24
Bubble levels, 73
Bucks
  approaching downed, 78
  bedding areas preferred by, 8, 13, 14
  bedding with does, 93

feeding areas preferred by, 9
growling vs. grunting, 66
locating nocturnal, 89–91
snow-tracking mature, 110–114
staging areas preferred by, 31
terrain features favored by, 13

C

Cables, quieting noise of, 37
Calls/calling
  adding realism to, 64–65
  attaching devices, 68
  decoys and, 64
  digital deer, 67, 68, 69–70
  doubling up, 64, 65
  early season strategies, 61–63
  frequency of, 63–64
  giving estrous doe bleats, 53, 63
  giving fawn bleats, 25, 63
  late season strategies, 124
  masking noise with, 106
  modifications, 66–70
  most successful types of calls, 61
  nocturnal bucks, 91
  peak of rut strategies, 94, 95, 96–97
  rattling, 70–71
  response time to, 62
  specialty, 65–66
  water-tracking strategies, 119
Cameras, 43–45
Camouflage
  for bowhunters' equipment, 102
  clothing for, 36, 101, 102
  cream, 36, 101
  man-made, 22–23
  natural, 20–22
  orange clothing and, 38, 98–99, 100
  during pre-season scouting, 47
  shooting lanes, 32
  snow camo clothing, 129
  tree stand construction and, 32
  using storms as, 55, 107
Canoes, types of, 115–116
Cellar holes, 23
Chasing, when to, 57
Clear-cuts, 19, 59
Clicking noise, 65
Clothing
  boots
    caring for, 126

Flagging tape, 99
Fluorescent orange clothing, importance of, 38
Forest debris, using for scent control, 39, 42
Fox urine
  on boots, 48
  on drag along pads, 34

G

Gear, securing, 38
GlenDel Buck targets, 29
Gloves, 36, 40
Golf carts, 32
Gore-tex boots, 40
Ground scents, 41–42
Growling, 66
Grunts
  making successful, 52
  during peak of rut, 94
  testing tubes, 62, 66
  tube adjustments, 67
  tube size and, 66
Guns. *See Firearms*
Gun wobble, 79

H

Handmade tree stands, safety of, 38
Hands, keeping warm, 127
Harnesses, quieting noise of, 37
Hats, 40, 127
Head nets, 101
Heat sensors for trail cameras, 45
Hickory nuts, 19
Highway medians, 23

I

In-field scouting, 11
Islands, 14

K

Kevlar canoes, 116

L

Landmarks and measuring distances, 31
Laser Bore Alignment kits, 80
Laser range finders, 31
Late season
  bedding areas, 14, 123
  calls, 124
  feeding, 120, 122, 123, 129
  lures, 122–123
  promising terrain features, 121–122
  scrapes and scrape lines, 121
  site location of tree stand in, 56

still-hunting, 121
tree stand placement, 25
using decoys, 124
validity of doe tags, 25
Lay of the land
  changes in, 10
  learning, 13
  understanding, 7
Leftover lumber, using, 38
Location preparation, 11
Logging roads, 132, 133
Lures
  in freezing weather, 130
  handling, 40
  in late season, 122–123
  placing, 41
  types to use, 57

M

Machinery, abandoned, 22–23
Man-made camouflage, 22–23
Man-made openings, 15
Mittens, 127
Mock scrapes, 52
Moon and rutting behavior, 88
Motion detectors for trail cameras, 45
Mountain laurel, 21

N

Natural camouflage, 20–22
Nocturnal bucks, locating, 89–91
Noise
  avoiding making patterns of, 48
  to bring buck into view, 56
  listening for deer, 104
  quieting cables, harnesses and wires, 37
  quivers and, 102
  of stands dampening, 37
  testing for, 37
  when leaving, 26
  using calls to mask, 106
  of vehicles, 32, 49
  when walking, 48
  when water-tracking, 116, 117
Non-rutting buck urine, using, 52
Nut production, 8

O

Off-season, using trail cameras during, 45
Open areas, 15, 113
Orchards, 19
Other hunters, signs of, 134

P

Peak of rut season
  ambush sites, 58, 87
  calling strategies, 94, 95, 96–97
  feeding locations, 87, 93
  finding does, 92–97
  locating breeding trails, 88
  locating nocturnal bucks, 89–91
  tips, 87–88
Peep sights, 81
Permanent tree stands, drawbacks to, 27
Plateaus, 14–15
Polyethylene canoes, 115, 116
Post season scouting, 46, 131–135
Pre-rut season
  bedding areas preferred by bucks, 13, 14
  feeding locations, 51
  rattling during, 71
  rubs/rub lines during, 52
  signs of, 50, 51
  signs of ending of, 55
  still-hunting, 54

Q

Quivers
  noise from, 102
  spraying with scent eliminators, 40

R

Raccoon urine on boots, 48
Racks, gauging number of points, 9
Range finders, 31, 52, 75
Rattling, 70–71
Ravines and travel routes, 16
Reed-assembly calls, 66
Ribbon trails, blaze orange for, 99
Rifles. *See Firearms*
Routines, adjusting to avoid human contact, 23
Royalex canoes, 116
Rubber boots, 11, 42, 47
Rubs/rub lines
  during early season, 9
  nocturnal bucks and, 91
  during peak of rut, 88, 93
  during pre-rut, 52
  reading, 32
  reappearance of, 50
  setting up trail cameras along, 44
Rut season
  bedding along stone walls, 23
  finding breeding trails, 88
  finding signs, 9

Tree stands
  approaching, 25, 27, 29, 34, 47
  best shield trees, 36
  brush removal and, 24
  camouflaging, 27, 28, 30
  when constructing, 32
  when not in use, 30
  checking out before using, 28, 38
  comfort, 25
  constructing, 12, 32, 35
  entering and exiting, 25, 26, 32
  flagging tape around, 99
  frequency of using, 26, 47
  height of, 25, 29, 36
  noise
  dampening to control, 37
  testing for, 37
  in off-season, 12, 57
  positioning, 26, 52
  safety and, 38
  shooting distances for bowhunters
    and, 52
  site location, 35, 36
  alternatives, 26, 34
  keeping secret, 25, 29
  during late season, 25, 56
  season and, 33
  time of day and, 34

  using last season's scrape line, 55
  winds and, 33–34
  tips for bowhunters, 28–31
  tips for firearm hunters, 33–38
  using another's, 25
  using in cold weather, 128
  using screw-in steps, 29

U
Utility lines, 59

V
Vandalism, 38
Vegetation, thick, 16
Vehicles
  leaving, 25
  parking, 29
  quieting noise of, 32, 49
Velvet removal, finding signs of, 91

W
Walking
  bobbing and weaving, 26
  body language when, 46
  sneaking techniques, 104
  speed when snow-tracking, 114
  speed when still-hunting, 106, 107,
    108

  using stop-and-go rhythm, 49, 103
Water-tracking
  ambushes, 119
  canoe types for, 115–116
  going to far side of body of water, 59
  islands and, 14
  noise when, 116, 117
  safety when, 116–117, 118
  secret buck trails and, 83
  still-hunting and, 119
  travel routes and, 16
Wildflowers, 21
Winds
  approaching tree stands and, 25, 29
  having alternative tree stands ready
    and, 26
  scent control and, 42, 47
  tree stand sitting and, 33–34
  in uneven terrain, 13
  using for scent control, 104, 105
working crosswinds, 105, 106
Winter
  bedding areas, 17
  setting up trail cameras during, 44
Wires, quieting noise of, 37

PHOTO CREDITS

Creative Publishing international
Your Complete Source of How-to Information for the Outdoors

Hunting Books
* Advanced Turkey Hunting
* Advanced Whitetail Hunting
* Beginner's Guide to Birdwatching
* Black Bear Hunting
* Bowhunting Equipment & Skills
* Bowhunter's Guide to Accurate Shooting
* The Complete Guide to Hunting
* Dog Training
* Elk Hunting
* How to Think Like a Survivor
* Hunting Record-Book Bucks
* Mule Deer Hunting
* Muzzleloading
* Outdoor Guide to Using Your GPS
* Waterfowl Hunting
* Whitetail Addicts Manual
* Whitetail Hunting
* Whitetail Techniques & Tactics
* Wild Turkey

Fishing Books
* Advanced Bass Fishing
* The Art of Freshwater Fishing

* The Complete Guide to Freshwater Fishing
* Fishing for Catfish
* Fishing Tips & Tricks
* Fishing with Artificial Lures
* Inshore Salt Water Fishing
* Kids Gone Campin'
* Kids Gone Fishin'
* Kids Gone Paddlin'
* Largemouth Bass
* Live Bait Fishing
* Modern Methods of Ice Fishing
* Northern Pike & Muskie
* Panfish
* Salt Water Fishing Tactics
* Smallmouth Bass
* Striped Bass Fishing: Salt Water Strategies
* Successful Walleye Fishing
* Ultralight Fishing

Fly Fishing Books
* The Art of Fly Tying + CD-ROM
* Complete Photo Guide to Fly Fishing

* Complete Photo Guide to Fly Tying
* Fishing Dry Flies
* Fly-Fishing Equipment & Skills
* Fly Fishing for Beginners
* Fly Fishing for Trout in Streams
* Fly-Tying Techniques & Patterns

Cookbooks
* All-Time Favorite Game Bird Recipes
* America's Favorite Fish Recipes
* America's Favorite Wild Game Recipes
* Backyard Grilling
* Cooking Wild in Kate's Kitchen
* Dressing & Cooking Wild Game
* The New Cleaning & Cooking Fish
* Preparing Fish & Wild Game
* The Saltwater Cookbook
* Venison Cookery
* The Wild Butcher
* The Wild Fish Cookbook
* The Wild Game Cookbook

To purchase these or other Creative Publishing international titles,
contact your local bookseller, or visit our website at
www.creativepub.com

  *The Complete* **FLY FISHERMAN**™